The Social Message of Mahayana Buddhism

"Engaged Buddhists" have attracted world-wide attention in the 21st century. They are carrying on non-violent struggles in different regions of the world, for promoting democracy, justice and human rights. This book provides answers to frequently asked questions that have been extracted from two of the main scriptures of Mahayana Buddhism viz. The Lotus Sutra and Shantideva's Bodhicaryavatara, which have inspired most of the "engaged Buddhists".

Other Books by Satya P. Agarwal

1. The Social Role of the Gita: How and Why
2. The Social Message of the Gita Symbolized as Lokasamgraha
3. तुलसी रामायण - जगमंगल-परायण
4. मानस एवं गीता - लोकमंगल-गुञ्जिता
5. लोकसंग्रहसन्देश:
6. The Gita and Tulasi-Ramayana : Their Common Call for the Good of All
7. Selections from the Mahabharata
8. The Gita for the 21st Century
9. छात्रोपयोगी भगवद्गीता
10. श्रीमद्भागवत का ज्ञान
11. The World Peace Agenda
12. Apad Dharma in the Mahabharata

Satya P. Agarwal
Ph.D. (University of California, Berkeley)

Urmila Agarwal
M.A. (University of the Pacific)

THE SOCIAL MESSAGE OF MAHAYANA BUDDHISM

FIRST EDITION

New Age Books
New Delhi (India)

THE SOCIAL MESSAGE OF MAHAYANA BUDDHISM

Published by
NEW AGE BOOKS
A-44, Naraina Industrial Area, Phase-I
New Delhi–110 028 (INDIA)
E-mail: nab@newagebooksindia.com
Website: www.newagebooksindia.com

ISBN: 978-81-7822-384-1

First Indian Edition: Delhi, 2012

Distributors
Urmila Agarwal
11293 Ridermark Row
Columbia MD 21044
Tel.: USA-410-997-7175
Email: ishamaya@erols.com

Printed and published by
RP Jain for New Age Books
A-44, Naraina Industrial Area
Phase-1, New Delhi 110 028. India

To

Alan Watts,
Eminent Buddhist Scholar
and
Joan Bondurant,
Eminent Gandhian Scholar
To our close association with them
in the 1950s, we trace the idea
of the present book

Contents

Preface

The conceptual origin of this book is linked with the study and research that we did in USA from 1953 onward. Alan Watts laid open before us the vast field of research opportunities connected with Buddhism. He arranged for us a short visit to the famous Buddhist Meditation centers of Kyoto (Japan). Also, the American Academy of Asian Studies (headed by Alan Watts) facilitated our cultural interaction with the Chinese community of San Francisco, in the context of their project aimed at building a Buddhist temple. For the multi-lingual Dharmic text to be used in this temple, the Sanskrit-section was prepared by us.

Simultaneously, our desire to do innovative research on Gandhi and Vinoba was strengthened through our close collaboration with Joan Bondurant who wrote "Conquest of Violence: The Gandhian Philosophy of Conflict". One of our own studies on "Sarvodaya" (The Gandhian Vision of Uplift of All) was completed in 1956, but it could not be sent for publication due to organisational red-tape.

Our research on "Lokasamgraha" (Good of the world) — which has similarities with Sarvodaya—picked up steam in 1987 (after we had completed our assignment with the United Nations). A strong fillip to this research was provided by the University of California, Berkeley, in 1991, when they made us a part of their Center for South Asia Studies. Our first book on Lokasamgraha was published in 1993, under the title "The Social Role of the Gita: How and Why." The main finding of this book, viz. that the social message of

"Bhagavad-Gita" is Lokasamgraha, received strong support from Gandhian scholars as well as university professors. This prompted us to extend the coverage of our research to books which have been influenced by Bhagavad-Gita.

In the year 2000, we published "The Gita and Tulasi-Ramayana: Their Common Call for the Good of All," in which we brought out the similarity between the social message of Bhagavad-Gita and that of Tulasi-Ramayana (a sixteenth-century Hindi text).

While looking for other texts that we could include in our research program, we came across Dr. Radhakrishnan's remark (made in 1948) that the most important Mahayana text (The Lotus Sutra) is indebted to Bhagavad-Gita. In fact, quite independently of this remark, we had started research on the social message of the Lotus Sutra. This research inevitably meant taking a close look at the important phenomenon of "Engaged Buddhism". In this process, we discovered that, while many of the "engaged Buddhists" had been inspired by the Lotus Sutra, some of them had been inspired by Shantideva's Bodhicaryavatara. The outcome of the consequent enlargement of the scope of our research is presented in this book.

In all our studies related to the social message of different texts, we have adopted a respectful attitude, because we do not want to hurt the feelings of those for whom these are scriptural texts. If any lapse has inadvertently occurred, we hope the readers will draw our attention to it so that we can take care of the problem (if any) in the next edition.

SATYA P. AGARWAL
URMILA AGARWAL

Acknowledgements

We have dedicated this book to Alan Watts and Joan Bondurant, who inspired us nearly sixty years ago. Although those two "great souls" are not with us now, the inspiration that they gave was a source of great encouragement as we planned and drafted this book. Another "great soul" who provided unflinching moral support to our research project, viz. Rakshpal Aggarwal, left this world suddenly in June 2011.

Valuable feedback at the time of finalization of the draft came informally from close friends, viz, Dr. Sham Narula, Dr. Rajan Narayanan, Dr. Satish Misra, Dr. R.S. Dwivedi, Dr. Pooran and Kusum Shukla, Santosh Aggarwal, Jaishriben, and Ila Desai.

Within our own family, our son Nishkam's role has been unique—he made available to us the literature that we needed, including the Sanskrit texts of the Lotus Sutra and Bodhicaryavatara. Technical and moral support came from all the members of the family, viz. Nishkam, Kokila, Seema, David, Isha, Kiran, Priya and Maya. Close relatives who rendered valuable help include Harish and Vinod Kashyap, Madan Mohan and Shashi Agarwal, Prabhat and Ambika Agarwal, Arun and Ritu Gupta, Veena and Anil Kumar, Manju and Dhanendra Kumar, Renu Mital, Dr. K.M. Mital, Rakesh and Alka Mital, Anil Narang, Savita and Anil Agarwal, and Abhay Bhushan. To all of them as well as to many others who rendered help but whose names are not specifically mentioned (in order to keep this list short), we express our sincere thankfulness.

Columbia, Maryland
October 2, 2011

SATYA P. AGARWAL
URMILA AGARWAL

CHAPTER 1

The Purpose and Plan of the Book

1.1 "Engaged Buddhism" is currently a popular subject of study and research. Several writers have brought to light, details of socially useful work done in the world, by scholars and activists who are Buddhists. References to Mahatma Gandhi (although he was not a Buddhist) are also made in such writings. It is abundantly clear that Ahimsa (non-violence) is one of the key elements of "engaged Buddhism".

1.2 Those who read the fascinating stories of "engaged Buddhists" often ask: what are the sources of their inspiration? Does the inspiration come primarily from Buddhist texts? Or do modern ideas, not necessarily connected with religion, also play a significant role? Similar questions were raised in respect of Gandhi, and he stated that, not only Bhagavad-Gita, but also several other books and individuals had inspired him.

1.3 Max Muller brought out, during the last two decades of the nineteenth century, fifty volumes of translations of religious texts, under the title "Sacred Books of the East". Volume 8 of that series included Bhagavad-Gita and Volume 21 was devoted to Saddharmapundarika (also called "The Lotus Sutra"). Bhagavad-Gita was translated from Sanskrit to English by K.T. Telang, and Saddharmapundarika was similarly translated from Sanskrit to English by J.H. Kern.

1.4 The Lotus Sutra is the most important, as well as the most ancient, text of Mahayana Buddhism. This text is undoubtedly the main source of inspiration of many of the "engaged Buddhists".

1.5 One is tempted to notice that the important role played by Bhagavad-Gita in Gandhi's life seems to be parallel to the important role played by the Lotus Sutra in the lives of many of the "engaged Buddhists." Since the work done by Gandhi, on the one hand, and "engaged Buddhists," on the other, have common features, a question naturally arises: Are there common features between Bhagavad-Gita and the Lotus Sutra? We will be in a position to answer this question in the last chapter of this book.

1.6 We as researchers specializing in modern trends in Hinduism and Buddhism have made an in-depth study of Bhagavad-Gita as well as of the Lotus Sutra. We published (in 1993) the results of the former study under the title "The Social Role of the Gita: How and Why", and feel encouraged to have received congratulatory messages from Gandhian and other scholars world-wide.

1.7 But why did we not publish so far, the results of our study of "The Lotus Sutra"? This delay can be accounted for, by our discovery, that some of the "engaged Buddhists" have been inspired primarily by Shantideva's book "Bodhicaryavatara". Therefore, we decided to expand our study, in the sense, that both "The Lotus Sutra" and "Bodhicaryavatara" should be covered together (rather than publish the results pertaining to "The Lotus Sutra" by itself).

1.8 Having decided that the two books should be studied together, we had to consider which aspects of the two texts should be looked into. We felt that the pattern of study that we had adopted in the case of Bhagavad-Gita (and which has given us so much success) was the most appropriate. This meant doing two things. First, to identify those portions of the two texts which, in our opinion, give the social message, that is, the message that has inspired "engaged Buddhists". Secondly, to identify those portions of the two texts, which give methods of implementing the social message. In our opinion, a knowledge of the methods can enable "engaged Buddhists" to make their contribution most effectively.

1.9 In the light of the above, the primary purpose of the present book is: firstly, to share with the readers, selected passages from the Lotus Sutra and Bodhicaryavatara, which, in our opinion, give the social message of Mahayana Buddhism, and secondly, to give the methods of implementing the social message. A subsidiary purpose of the book is indicated in the next para.

1.10 The social message and the methods of implementing it, together constitute the "textual evidence" derived from the two books (accounting for nearly three-fourths of the present book). Illustrative material of an historical nature has been added by reviewing briefly what the Mahayana-influenced Asian countries have done by way of follow-up action. We call this "historical review" a subsidiary purpose of the present book - and we use the word "subsidiary" because the review that we present is very short.

1.11 The plan of the book can now be specified. Chapter Two conveys to the readers, in a summary form, the content of each chapter of the Lotus Sutra as well as Bodhicaryavatara. Chapter Three explains, with the help of selected passages from both the books, what their social message is. Chapter Four specifies, again with the help of selected passages from both the books, five types of methods that can be used for implementing the social message. Chapter Five tells briefly about the important role that the Chinese people played in keeping alive, and exporting, the multi-faceted Mahayana (which otherwise might have faced extinction due to its virtual disappearance from India). Chapter Six summarizes the nurturing and development of the social message, towards success in Japan. Chapter Seven narrates briefly how people of Korea, Vietnam and Taiwan faced challenges in their practice of Mahayana, but still managed to make their valuable contribution. Chapter Eight completes this short review of Asia-centered journey of Mahayana, by drawing attention to the difficulties faced by Nepal and Tibet. Finally, Chapter Nine gives a summary of the book and concluding remarks (which will include our opinion on the point raised in para 1.5).

CHAPTER 2

Two Main Sources of the Social Message

2.1 The basic source of the social message of Mahayana Buddhism is called "The Lotus Sutra". Although the exact date of preparation of this text (in India) is not known, it is generally believed to have been written during the first two centuries. Subsequently, during the eighth century, the social message was elaborated by Shantideva in his book "Bodhicaryavatara". In the present book, we will utilize both these sources, in order to obtain a demystified and comprehensive account of the meaning, scope, and methods of implementation of the social message of Mahayana.

The Lotus Sutra

2.2 During the last two decades of the nineteenth century, Max Muller (1823-1900) included "The Lotus Sutra" in the series of publications called "Sacred Books of the East." Jan Hendrik Kern used a Sanskrit text of the Lotus Sutra and translated it into English. Scholars feel that this text was probably not the original which was taken to China. The earliest extant Chinese translation was made by Dharmaraksa in 286 (revised 290). However, the Chinese version, which is commonly used now, is the translation done by Kumarajiva and his team, in 406.

2.3 The Sanskrit title of the text of the Lotus Sutra is "Saddharmapundarika Sutra". One way of translating this title into English is "The good dharma symbolized as lotus".

In the Indian tradition (i.e, Hindu as well as Buddhist), the lotus represents beauty, quality of rising up, and non-attachment. In China, Japan and other east-Asian countries, the Lotus Sutra has won the hearts of scholars as well as common people.

2.4 We have noticed that the Sanskrit text of the Lotus Sutra can, by careful editing, be given a shape that is fairly close to Kumarajiva's version. We feel that, for our present purpose, using such a Sanskrit text is preferable to depending entirely on the English translation.

A brief summary of the text.

2.5 The Lotus Sutra has twenty-eight chapters. A chapter-wise outline of the contents is given below:-

Chapter 1. Prologue. Preparing the scenario for the Buddha's address to the large gathering at Vulture Peak.

Chapter 2. Awakening of the Lord (i.e. the Buddha) from his mystic trance; the Lord's address which displays his transcendent skilfulness, proved by the apparent reference to three vehicles, whereas in reality there is but one vehicle.

Chapter 3. Prophecy of the Lord regarding the future destiny of Shariputra. Second turn of the wheel of the Dharma on that occasion, with incidental commemoration of the first turn near Varanasi. Parable of the burning house, to exemplify the skill of the good father in saving his children from the burning pains of mundane existence. Since this chapter explains the meaning of the ideal "Bodhisattva", a brief summary of that explanation is given here.

There are some who apply themselves to the commandment of the Tathagata to acquire the knowledge of the four noble truths, for the sake of their own complete Nirvana. Other beings apply themselves to the commandment of the Tathagata to learn to understand causes and effects, for the sake of their own complete Nirvana - they covet the vehicle of the Pratyekabuddhas.

Others again, desirous of the knowledge of the all-knowing, the knowledge of the Buddha, the knowledge of the self-born one, apply themselves to the commandment of the Tathagata to learn to understand the knowledge, powers, and freedom of the Tathagata, for the sake of the common weal and happiness, out of compassion to the world, for the benefit, weal, and happiness of the world at large, both gods and men, for the sake of the complete Nirvana of all beings. Therefore they are called Bodhisattvas Mahasattvas.

Chapter 4. Another parable, exemplifying the skill of the wise father in leading a child who has gone astray and lost all self-respect, back to a feeling of his innate nobility and to happiness.

Chapter 5. Parable of the plants and the rain, to exemplify the impartiality and equal care of the Lord for all creatures. Parable of the blind man, to intimate that the phenomena have but an apparent reality, and that the ultimate goal of all endeavours must be to reach all-knowingness.

Chapter 6. Sundry predictions as proofs of the power of the Lord to look into the future.

Chapter 7. The Lord has knowledge of the past too, for example, his remembrance of the turning of the wheel of Dharma by the Tathagata Mahabhijnajnanabhibhu. Edifying history of the sixteen sons of this Tathagata.

Chapter 8. Prophecy regarding five hundred Arhats.

Chapter 9. Prophecy regarding Ananda, Rahula, and two thousand monks.

Chapter 10. The Lord teaches how pious preachers of the Dharma, who will come in after-times, ought to be duly honored, and promises that he will always protect them.

Chapter 11. Display of the miraculous power of Shakyamuni shown in the appearance of a Stupa, which, being opened by him, discloses to sight, the frame of the expired Tathagata Prabhutaratna, who is desirous of hearing the exposition of the Lotus Sutra. How Shakyamuni in a former birth strove to acquire the Lotus Sutra.

Chapter 12. Although Devadatta's conduct in his present life was full of blemishes, the Buddha says that he was a great person in his earlier life. Furthermore, the Buddha, recognizing his earlier obligations to Devadatta, announces that, in an age to come, Devadatta will become a Tathagata named Devaraja. Another special feature of this chapter is about the wise daughter of the Naga-king, who, only eight years of age, attained enlightenment.

Chapter 13. The Lord's assurance to Gautami, Yashodhara, and the nuns that, in an age to come, they too will become Tathagatas. Another special feature of this chapter is that hosts of disciples and Bodhisattvas promise to take up the difficult task of preaching the Lotus Sutra, after the Lord's Nirvana.

Chapter 14. Practical rules for the conduct of the preachers, in and out of society. Parable of the king who rewards his valiant warriors–in the same manner, the Buddha will reward those who struggle for his sake, by bestowing upon them all kinds of favors, and culminating in Enlightenment.

Chapter 15. Splendid vision of innumerable Bodhisattvas evoked by the creative power of the Lord. Long pause during which the Tathagata and the four classes of hearers are silent. Perplexity of Maitreya on hearing that the innumerable Bodhisattvas have all been the pupils of the Lord.

Chapter 16. The Lord explains to Maitreya and others, by revealing the immense duration of his lifetime, in the past as well as in the future.

Chapter 17. Meritoriousness of the belief in the immense duration of the Tathagatas and all those who have once become Buddhas.

Chapter 18. The Lord details the great merit attending a ready acceptance of the preaching of the Dharma.

Chapter 19. Exposition of the advantages, worldly as well as spiritual, enjoyed by the preachers of the Lotus Sutra.

Chapter 20. Story of Sadaparibhuta, exemplifying the superiority of simple-mindedness and pure-heartedness to worldly wisdom and scepticism.

Chapter 21. Grand show exhibited by the two Tathagatas Shakyamuni and Prabhutaratna conjointly. Pause after the performance. After the pause, a great stir amongst gods, celestial and infernal beings, men, etc. Shakyamuni extols the Lotus Sutra in which the true Dharma is succinctly taught, as well as those who will preach this Sutra after the departure of the Lord.

Chapter 22. The Buddha asks Bodhisattvas to preach the Dharma to all beings. The Bodhisattvas, headed by Visistacaritra, gladly accept to fulfill the command of the Tathagata.

Chapter 23. Self-sacrifice of the Bodhisattva Sarvasattvapriyadarsana, otherwise called Bhaisajyaraja. Glorification of the Lotus Sutra.

Chapter 24. Visit of the Bodhisattva Gadgadasvara to the Saha-world. Extraordinary qualities and achievements of Gadgadasvara, narrated by the Tathagata. Glorification of the meditation called "Sarvarupasandarsana".

Chapter 25. Grandeur and omnipresence of Avalokitesvara. Those who pray to him, receive full protection from all difficulties.

Chapter 26. Efficacy of talismanic spells (Dharanis).

Chapter 27. Wonderful and edifying story of the conversion of King Subhavyuha, through the instrumentality of his wife Vimaladatta, and of the two sons named Vimalagarbha and Vimalanetra. Glorification of eight forms of meditation.

Chapter 28. Bodhisattva Samantabhadra charges himself with the task of being a protector to the preachers of the Lotus Sutra, in after-times i.e, after the departure of Shakyamuni.

Shantideva's book "Bodhicaryavatara"

2.6 Shantideva (685-763) was a Mahayana monk who spent considerable time at Nalanda University. The Sanskrit title of his book is "Bodhicaryavatara" which can be translated as "Entering the Path of Enlightenment." A copy of the book reached Tibet (shortly after it was written) where it was translated, but it seems that no Chinese translation was made at that time. Among modern leaders of "engaged Buddhism", the 14th Dalai Lama has acknowledged his indebtedness to this book.

A brief summary of the text

2.7 Shantideva's book "Bodhicaryavatara" has ten chapters. His primary object is to instruct the readers in the moral, devotional and mental techniques which can transform them into Bodhisattvas, the saviors of all beings. A chapter-wise outline of the contents of the book is given below:-

Chapter 1. Shantideva says that the aspirant should feel happy when the "Thought of Enlightenment" has arisen in him. Shantideva distinguishes between the mind resolved upon awakening, and the mind that has actually proceeded towards awakening. He puts it this way : the initial resolution creates merit, but the merit of the bodhisattva-aspirant who has actually started the journey towards awakening, has no limit.

Chapter 2. Shantideva says that the aspirant should be aware of his strengths and weaknesses, particularly the latter. He therefore advises that the aspirant should confess his weaknesses before the Buddha: "May the Lord accept my confession and transgression. That which was not good, Lord, will not be done again by me."

Chapter 3. Shantideva says that the aspirant should pray to the Buddha to make him fit to serve needy people in the world : May I be an imperishable treasury for needy beings. May I have the strength to stand in order to do what is beneficial in every possible way. With rains of food and drink, may I dispel the anguish of hunger and thirst.

Chapter 4. Shantideva says that the aspirant should strengthen his resolve to do good to people who need help: Their minds fixed upon the means of livelihood, fishermen, outcastes, farmers, and the like, prevail over the misfortunes of cold, heat, and similar difficulties. Why shall I not prevail in the work of the world's well-being? If I do not do good when I am capable of goodness, what will I do when I am stupefied by the sorrows of an evil destiny?

Chapter 5. Shantideva is not satisfied with the traditional practice of giving dana (charity): If the perfection of charity could have made the world free from poverty, it must not have been an attribute of the saviors, since even today there is poverty in the world. The obvious message is that the system itself, which creates poverty, must be changed. In other words, a mental revolution is needed : By the mere thought of forsaking all of our possessions for the sake of all creatures, along with the consequent merit of this great act, the perfection of charity is proclaimed. It is thus a mental apparatus.

Chapter 6. Shantideva's plea for ksanti (patience) touches every one's heart : Those who cause me suffering, are like Buddhas bestowing their blessings, since they lead me to liberating paths. Why should I get angry with them? Don't they obstruct your virtuous practice? No! There is no virtuous practice greater than patience. Therefore I will never get angry with those who cause me suffering. If, because of my own shortcomings, I do not practice patience with my enemy, it is not he, but I, who prevents me from practicing patience. Obviously, Shantideva is formulating a non-violent approach to tackle problems of inter-personal relationships.

Chapter 7. One of the consequences of cultivating patience is complete fearlessness, and moving further on from there, Shantideva pleads for heroic strength (Virya): The delight of the Dharma is the most noble course of endless delight; there is nothing to compare to it. The false pleasure of arrogance and derision, which only causes sorrow, not delight, is of no value when compared with the nobility of virya - a quality to be described in terms of self-mastery, courage, strength, and order, which, in turn, is linked with identity and exchange of one's self with another.

Chapter 8. The topic of this chapter is dhyana (meditation), but Shantideva's meditation is of a special type : First of all, I should make an effort to meditate upon the equality between my self and others. So I should protect all beings as I do myself, because we are all equal in wanting pleasure and not wanting pain. Hence I should dispel the misery of others, because it is suffering just like my own. And I should benefit others, because they are sentient beings, just like myself. When both myself and others are similar in that we wish to be happy, then what is so special about me? Why do I strive for my happiness alone?

Chapter 9. In this chapter, which is entitled "Prajna-paramita" (Perfection of Wisdom), Shantideva defends Madhyamika beliefs against a multitude of objections from Buddhist as well as non-Buddhist philosophies. Since our interest in this book is primarily related to the social message, we have not considered it necessary to utilize the philosophical arguments contained in this chapter.

Chapter 10. This last chapter of the book is a masterpiece, containing fifty-eight verses. The first three verses give us an idea of the sublime spirit of Shantideva's dedication to the cause of "good of the world" : Whatever benefit is mine from creating this Introduction to the way of enlightenment, by it may all beings become ornaments in the way of enlightenment. Let as many beings as there are in all places, who are suffering pain of body or of thought, obtain by my merits, oceans of happiness and of joy. As long as there is samsara, may there be no loss of happiness to people in any way. May the world unceasingly obtain the happiness of the Bodhisattva.

Chapter 3

Spiritual as well as Secular Aspects of the Message

3.1 In the preceding chapter, we introduced the two books – the Lotus Sutra and Bodhicaryavatara – on the basis of which we will now specify the social message of Mahayana Buddhism. Although both these books are religious texts, their message is not confined to spiritual matters. In fact, secular issues affecting the day-to-day worldly life of common people are also highlighed, along with Dharma, in both the books.

Social Message

3.2 In our opinion, the social message of Mahayana Buddhism is: "Contribute to the good of the world", the complete meaning of which is obtained by looking at the message together with four sub-messages:-

(i) Bodhisattva-based ideal

Bodhisattva, rather than Arhat or Pratyekabuddha, should be the ideal to be attained in human life, because Bodhisattva's aim is "good of the world". "Concentration on Bodhisattva" is the "eka-yana" (Single Vehicle) of Mahayana Buddhism.

(ii) Spiritual as well as secular

The "good of the world" includes spiritual advancement of all as well as satisfaction of their basic needs like food, health and education.

(iii) No discrimination

All human beings should have the assurance of equality of treatment, free from discrimination on any ground like sex, age and socio-economic status. In particular, the status of women, in regard to their education, health, and participation in religion, should be equal to that of men.

(iv) Reform rather than punish

Wherever evil-minded, anti-social persons exist in the society, they should be reformed rather than punished. This means adherence to Ahimsa (non-violence)

Textual evidence

3.3 For the social message, and for each of the four sub-messages, we have identified relevant portions of the two books. Our presentation of each of these passages includes the text in Sanskrit as well as its simple meaning in English.

Good of the world : Selections from Lotus Sutra (or LS)

3.4 प्रयता सुचित्ता भवथा कृतांजलि
भाषिष्यते लोकहितानुकम्पी।
वर्षिष्यते धर्ममनन्तवर्षम्
तर्पिष्यते ये स्थित बोधिहेतोः।। LS 1.99

prayata sucitta bhavatha kritanjali
bhasisyate lokahitanukampi
varsisyate dharmamanatavarsam
tarpisyate ye sthita bodhihetoh —*LS 1.99*

Simple meaning—Be attentive and adopt a prayerful posture, because the compassionate Lord is going to preach for the good of the world. He will bring down the never-ending rain of Dharma, and enliven all the aspirants. LS 1.99

3.5 येऽपि तु शारिपुत्र अतीतध्वन्यभूवन् दशसु दिक्ष्वप्रमेयेष्वसंख्येषु लोकधातुषु तथागता अर्हन्तः सम्यक्सम्बुद्धा बहुजनहिताय बहुजनसुखाय लोकानुकम्पायै महतो जनकायस्यार्थाय हिताय सुखाय देवानां च मनुष्याणां च धर्मं देशितवन्तः।। LS Chapter 2 ye'pi tu sariputra atita' dhvanyabhuvan dasasu diksvaprameyesvasamkhyesu lokadhatusu tathagata arhantah samyaksambuddha bahujanahitaya bahujanasukhaya lokanukampayai mahato janakayasyarthaya hitaya sukhaya devanam ca manusyanam ca dharmam desitavantah.

LS Chapter 2

Simple meaning–Sariputra, all the Tathagatas, the Arhats, and the Perfectly Enlightened, existed in times past and preached Dharma, in countless, innumerable spheres in all directions, for the good of all, for the happiness of all, out of mercy to the world, for the benefit of gods as well as men.

LS Chapter 2

3.6 येऽपि तु शारिपुत्र अनागतेऽध्वनि भविष्यन्ति दशसु
दिक्ष्वप्रमेयेष्वसंख्येषु लोकधातुषु तथागता अर्हन्तः
सम्यक्सम्बुद्धा बहुजनहिताय बहुजनसुखाय लोकानुकम्पायै
महतो जनकायस्यार्थाय हिताय सुखाय देवानां च
मनुष्याणां च धर्मं देशयिष्यन्ति ।। LS Chapter 2

ye'pi tu sariputra anagate'dhvani bhavisyanti dasasu diksvaprameyesvasamkhyesu lokadhatusu tathagata arhantah samyaksambuddha bahujanahitaya bahujanasukhaya lokanukampayai mahato janakayasyarthaya hitaya sukhaya devanam ca manusyanam ca dharmam desayisyanti

—*LS Chapter 2*

Simple meaning—Sariputra, all the Tathagatas, the Arhats, and the Perfectly Enlightened, will exist in future and will preach Dharma, in countless, innumerable spheres in all directions, for the good of all, for the happiness of all, out of mercy to the world, for the benefit of gods as well as men.

LS Chapter 2

3.7 इयं शारिपुत्र मम धर्ममुद्रा
या पश्चिमे कालि मयाद्य भाषिता ।
हिताय लोकस्य सदेवकस्य
दिशासु विदिशासु च देशयस्व ।। LS 3.105

iyam sariputra mama dharmamudra
ya pascime kali mayadya bhasita
hitaya lokasya sadevakasya
disasu vidisasu ca desayasva // —*LS 3.105*

Simple meaning—This, Sariputra, is the closing word of my Dharma, which now at the last time I pronounce for the good of the world, including the gods. Preach it in all quarters. LS 3.105

3.8 इयं सदा लोकहिताय धर्मता
तर्पेति धर्मेणिमु सर्वलोकम्।
संतर्पितश्चाप्यथ सर्वलोक:
प्रमुंचते ओषधि पुष्पकाणि।। LS 5.38

iyam sada lokahitaya dharmata
tarpeti dharmenimu sarvalokam
santarpitascapyatha sarvalokah
pramuncate osadhi puspakani —*LS 5.38*

Simple meaning—So it is the very nature of the Dharma to promote the everlasting good of the world; by the Dharma the whole world is recreated, and as the plants, when refreshed, expand their blossoms, the world does the same when refreshed. LS 5.38

3.9 देशयितु सुगतो धर्मं बहुजनहिताय बहुजनसुखाय
लोकानुकम्पायै महतो जनकायस्यार्थाय हिताय सुखाय
देवानां च मनुष्याणां च ।। LS Chapter 7

desayitu sugato dharmam bahujanahitaya
bahujanasukhaya lokanukampayai mahato
janakayasyarthaya hitaya sukhaya devanam ca
manusyanam ca —*LS Chapter 7*

Simple meaning—Preach the Dharma, O Sugata, for the good of all, for the happiness of all, out of compassion for the world, for the benefit of gods as well as men. LS Chapter 7

3.10 आश्चर्यभूतो जिन अप्रमेयो
उत्पन्न लोकस्मि हितानुकम्पी।

नाथोऽसि शास्तासि गुरूसि जातो
अनुगृहीता दशिमा दिशोऽद्य ।। LS 7.21

ascaryabhuto jina aprameyo
utpanna lokasmi hitanukampi
nathosi sastasi gurusi jato
anugrihita dasima disodya —*LS 7.21*

Simple meaning—O Wonderful, Matchless Buddha, so beneficial and compassionate, you have come to save the world. You are a protector, a ruler, a teacher, a master, today all quarters are blessed. LS 7.21

3.11 नमोऽस्तु ते अप्रतिमा महर्षे
देवातिदेवा कलविंकसुस्वरा।
विनायका लोकि सदेवकस्मिन्
वन्दामि ते लोकहितानुकम्पी ।। LS 7.31

namo'stu te apratima maharse
devatideva kalavinkasusvara
vinayaka loki sadevakasmin
vandami te lokahitanukampi —*LS 7.31*

Simple meaning—Homage to thee, matchless great Seer, chief god of gods, whose voice is sweet as the lark's. Leader in the world, doing good to all, I bow to thee, who art so benign and bounteous to the world. LS 7.31

3.12 साधु दर्शन बुद्धान लोकनाथान तायिनाम्।
त्रधातुकस्मि बुद्धा वै सत्त्वानां ये प्रमोचका: ।। LS 7.47

sadhu darsana buddhana lokanathana tayinam
tradhatukasmi buddha vai sattvanam ye pramocakah
—*LS 7.47*

Simple meaning—How glorious is the sight of the Buddhas, the mighty Lords of the world; those Buddhas who are to save all beings in this world. LS 7.47

3.13 दृष्टोऽसि लोकप्रद्योत सुचिरेणासि आगतः।
उत्पन्नु सर्वसत्त्वानां कृतेन अनुकम्पकः ।। LS 7.54
dristo'si lokapradyota sucirenasi agatah
utpannu sarvasattvanam kritena anukampakah
—LS 7.54

Simple meaning—Hail! thou art here at last, O Light of the world! thou art born to be bounteous towards all beings.
LS 7.54

3.14 अमितं च तस्यायु तदा भविष्यति।
यः स्थास्यते लोकहितानुकम्पकः ।। LS 9.4
amitam ca tasyayu tada bhavisyati
yah sthasyate lokahitanukampakah *—LS 9.4*

Simple meaning—The duration of the Lord's life will be immense. He will always be doing good to the world with infinite compassion. LS 9.4

3.15 अन्यत्र चिन्तेय सदा विचक्षणो
भवेय बुद्धोऽहमिमे च सत्त्वाः।
एतन्ममो सर्वसुखोपधानम्
यं धर्म श्रावेमि हिताय लोके ।। LS 14.35
anyatra cinteya sada vicaksano
bhaveya buddho' hamime ca sattvah
etanmamo sarvasukhopadhanam
yam dharma sravemi hitaya loke *—LS 14.35*

Simple meaning—The wise man is always thinking: How can I and all these beings become Buddhas? I will always preach this true Dharma, upon which the happiness of all beings as well as the good of the world depends. LS 14.35

3.16 तथैव बुद्धो अहु धर्मराजा
क्षान्तिबलः प्रज्ञप्रभूतकोशः।
धर्मेण शासामिमु सर्वलोकम्
हितानुकम्पी करुणायमानः ।। LS 14.51

tathaiva buddho ahu dharmaraja
ksantibalah prajnaprabhutakosah
dharmena sasamimu sarvalokam
hitanukampi karunayamanah —*LS 14.51*

Simple meaning—I, the Buddha, the Lord of Dharma, have infinite patience and a vast treasure of wisdom. I govern the whole world, doing good to all with infinite compassion. LS 14.51

3.17 यमेवाहं लोकपिता स्वयंभूः
चिकित्सकः सर्वप्रजान नाथः ।। LS 16.21
yamevaham lokapita svayambhuh
cikitsakah sarvaprajana nathah —*LS 16.21*

Simple meaning—The Lord said, "I am the father of the world, the self-born, the Healer who saves all and does good to all". LS 16.21

3.18 मूर्धेन च नमस्यन्ति अहमप्येदृशो भवेत्।
अनागतस्मिन्नध्वानि तारेयं प्राणिकोटयः ।। LS 17.33
murdhena ca namasyanti
ahamapyedriso bhavet
anagatasminnadhvani
tareyam pranikotayah —*LS 17.33*

Simple meaning—The aspirants bow their heads to the Bodhisattvas and pray: "May we also, in due course of time, become bodhisattvas, in order to ensure the welfare of all, as also the release of all from suffering''. LS 17.33

3.19 दृष्ट्वा च तं चिन्तयि तस्मि काले
गमिष्यते एष द्रुमस्य मूलम्।
बुधिष्यते बोधिमनुत्तरां शिवाम्
हिताय लोकस्य सदेवकस्य ।। LS 17.59
dristva ca tam cintayi tasmi kale
gamisyate esa drumasya mulam
budhisyate bodhimanuttaram sivam
hitaya lokasya sadevakasya —*LS 17.59*

Simple meaning—At the sight of such a man (who teaches Lotus Sutra), one may directly make the reflection that he is promoting the true Dharma, to arrive at blessed enlightenment, to do good to the world including gods.

LS 17.59

3.20 बुद्धाश्च ये लोकहितानुकम्पका:
सश्रावकास्तस्य निशाम्य घोषम्।
कुर्वन्ति रक्षां मुखदर्शनाय
तुष्टा भवन्ति ब्रुवतोऽस्य धर्मम् ।। LS 19.60
buddhasca ye lokahitanukampakah
sasravakastasya nisamya ghosam
kurvanti raksam mukhadarsanaya
tusta bhavanti bruvato'sya dharmam —*LS 19.60*

Simple meaning—The Buddhas, who always do good to the world with infinite compassion, on hearing the voice of the preacher, feel satisfied that he is preaching the true Dharma, and make sure that the preacher is protected. LS 19.60

3.21 अचिंतिया लोकहितानुधर्मता
अभिज्ञज्ञानास्ति प्रतिष्ठितानाम्।
ये ऋद्धि दर्शन्ति अनन्तचक्षुष:
प्रामोद्यहेतोरिह सर्वदेहिनाम् ।। LS 21.1
acintiya lokahitanudharmata
abhijnajnanasti pratisthitanam
ye riddhi darsanti anantacaksusah
pramodyahetoriha sarvadehinam —*LS 21.1*

Simple meaning—Inconceivable is the power to do good to the world, possessed by those who, firmly established in transcendent knowledge, by means of their unlimited vision, display their superhuman faculty, in order to gladden all living beings on earth. LS 21.1

3.22 त्राता खल्वपि अयं सद्धर्मपुण्डरीको धर्मपर्याय: सर्वसत्त्वानां
सर्वभयेभ्य: विमोचक: सर्वदु:खेभ्य: ।। LS chapter 23

trata khalvapi ayam saddharmapundariko dharmaparyayah sarvasattvanam sarvabhayebhyah vimocakah sarvaduhkhebhyah —*LS chapter 23*

Simple meaning—The Dharma of this Lotus Sutra saves all beings from fear and delivers them from grief too.
LS Chapter 23

3.23 साधु साधु समन्तभद्र यत्र हि नाम त्वमेवं बहुजनहिताय बहुजनसुखाय लोकानुकम्पायै महतो जनकायस्यार्थाय हिताय सुखाय प्रतिपन्नः ।। LS chapter 28

sadhu sadhu samantabhadra yatra hi nama tvamevam bahujanahitaya bahujanasukhaya lokanukampayai mahato janakayasyarthaya hitaya sukhaya pratipannah.
—*LS chapter 28*

Simple meaning—The Lord said, "Very well, very well, Samantabhadra. I am happy to see that you have dedicated yourself to promote the good of all and the happiness of all, out of compassion for the world, for the benefit of all."
LS Chapter 28

Good of the world : Selections from Bodhicaryavatara (or BCA)

3.24 पारम्पर्येण साक्षाद्वा सत्त्वार्थं नान्यदाचरेत् ।
सत्त्वानामेव चार्थाय सर्वं बोधाय नामयेत् ।। BCA 5.101

paramparyena saksadva sattvartham nanyadacaret
sattvanameva carthaya sarvam bodhaya namayet -
—*BCA 5.101*

Simple meaning—"Welfare of all" is the only goal to be achieved, both directly and indirectly. "Welfare" includes both spiritual and secular aspects. (Spiritual aspect is symbolized by "Bodhi", and secular aspect is symbolized by "loka-hita"). BCA 5.101

3.25 तथागताराधनमेतदेव
स्वार्थस्य संसाधनमेतदेव ।

लोकस्य दुःखापहमेतदेव
तस्मान्ममास्तु व्रतमेतदेव ।। BCA 6.127
tathagataradhanametadeva
svarthasya samsadhanametadeva
lokasya duhkhapahametadeva
tasmanmamastu vratametadeva —*BCA 6.127*

Simple meaning—For achieving the goal of "welfare of all," my immediate contribution is that I take a firm vow, viz. that I will try to destroy the sorrows of the world. I will view this as my worship of the Buddhas, and the source of my own happiness too. BCA 6.127

3.26 यथा गृहीतं सुगतैर्बोधिचित्तं पुरातनैः ।
तद्वदुत्पादयाम्येष बोधिचित्तं जगद्हिते ।। BCA 3.22-23
yatha grihitam sugatairboddhicittam puratanaih
tadvadutpadayamyesa bodhicittam jagadhite
—*BCA 3.22-23*

Simple meaning—Following the example of Bodhisattvas, I (i.e. all those who are Mahayana Buddhists) should direct bodhicitta (i.e. spiritual aspiration) to contribute to the cause of "good of the world". BCA 3.22-23

3.27 आकाशस्य स्थितिर्यावद् यावच्च जगतः स्थितिः ।
तावन्मम स्थितिर्भूयात् जगद् दुःखानि निघ्नतः ।। BCA 10.55
akasasya sthitiryavad yavacca jagatah sthitih
tavanmama sthitirbhuyad jagad duhkhani nighnatah
—*BCA 10.55*

Simple meaning—For as long as space endures, and for as long as living beings remain, until then may I too abide, to dispel the misery of the world. BCA 10.55

3.28 यत्किंचित् जगतो दुःखं तत्सर्वं मयि पच्यताम् ।
बोधिसत्त्वशुभैः सर्वैः जगत् सुखितमस्तु च ।। BCA 10.56
yatkincit jagato duhkham tatsarvam mayi pacyatam
bodhisattvasubhaih sarvaih jagat sukhitamastu ca
—*BCA 10.56*

Simple meaning—Whatever the sorrow of the world, may all that be absorbed by me, and may the world be comforted by all the glorious Bodhisattvas. BCA 10.56

3.29 मयान्यद् दुःखं हन्तव्यं दुःखत्वादात्मदुःखवत्।
अनुग्राह्या मयान्येऽपि सत्त्वत्वादात्मसत्त्ववत् ।। BCA 8.94

mayanyad dukham hantavyam
duhkhatvadatmaduhkhavat
anugrahya mayanyepi
sattvatvadatmasattvavat —*BCA 8.94*

Simple meaning—Another person's sorrow is to be destroyed by me because it is sorrow like my own. All other persons are to be honored by me because their self is like my own. BCA 8.94

3.30 अतः परार्थं कृत्वापि न मदो न च विस्मयः।
न विपाकफलाकांक्षा परार्थैकान्ततृष्णया ।। BCA 8.109

atah parartham kritvapi na mado na ca vismayah
na vipakaphalakanksa pararthaikantatrisnaya
—*BCA 8.109*

Simple meaning—After having done something for the benefit of others, let there be neither arrogance nor desire for recognition, nor desire for any benefit in return. Let there be only thirst for the other's benefit. BCA 8.109

3.31 आयातायात शीघ्रं भयमपनयत भ्रातरो जीविताः स्म
सम्प्राप्तोऽस्माकमेष ज्वलदभयकरः कोऽपि चीरीकुमारः।
सर्वं यस्यानुभावाद् व्यसनमपगतं प्रीतिवेगाः प्रवृत्ताः
जातं सम्बोधिचित्तं सकलजनपरित्राणमाता दया च ।। BCA 10.13

ayatayata sighram bhayamapanayata bhrataro jivitah sma
samprapto'smakamesa jvaladabhayakarah ko'pi cirikumarah
sarvam yasyanubhavad vyasanamapagatam pritivegah pravrittah
jatam sambodhicittam sakalajanaparitranamata daya ca
—*BCA 10.13*

Simple meaning—Come quickly, come fast, throw away all fear and live in peace, because Bodhisattva, the Prince of Peace, has arrived. He is also the compassionate Mother who saves all beings and removes all impurities. BCA 10.13

3.32 क्लेशस्वतंत्रो लोकोऽयं न क्षमः स्वार्थसाधने।
तस्मान्मयैषां कर्तव्यं नाशक्तोऽहं यथा जनः ।। BCA 7.50
klesasvatantro loko'yam na ksamah svarthasadhane
tasmanmayaisam kartavyam nasakto'ham yatha janah
—BCA 7.50

Simple meaning—Many people in the world are unable to achieve their own welfare. Therefore I (i.e. those who are Mahayana Buddhists and have the capability) should help those who are in need. BCA 7.50

3.33 काये नौबुद्धिमाधाय गत्यागमननिश्रयात्।
यथाकामं गमं कायं कुरु सत्त्वार्थसिद्धये BCA 5.70
kaye naubuddhimadhaya gatyagamananisrayat
yathakamam gamam kayam kuru sattvarthasiddhaye
—BCA 5.70

Simple meaning—After making the intellect, the driving force in the body, because it can come and go in a desired direction, make sure that the body moves in accordance with one's dedication, for the sake of the well-being of people. BCA 5.70

3.34 तस्मान्मयानपेक्षेण कायस्त्यक्तो जगद् हिते।
अतोऽयं बहुदोषोऽपि धार्यते कर्मभाण्डवत् ।। BCA 8.184
tasmanmayanapeksena kayastyakto jagadhite
ato'yam bahudoso'pi dharyate karmabhandavat
—BCA 8.184

Simple meaning—Willingly I offer my services for the welfare of the world. Henceforth my body is borne, although it has many faults, like an instrument of Karma in the service of all. BCA 8.184

3.35 अंगारतप्तोपलशस्त्रवृष्टिः
अद्यप्रभृत्यास्तु च पुष्पवृष्टिः।
तच्छस्त्रयुद्धं च परस्परेण
क्रीडार्थमद्यास्तु च पुष्पयुद्धम् ॥ BCA 10.9

angarataptopalasastravristih
adyaprabhrityastu ca puspavristih
tacchastrayuddham ca parasparena
kridarthamadyastu ca puspayuddham —BCA 10.9

Simple meaning—May the shower of swords, stones and burning charcoal, be henceforth a flower–rain, and the unceasing battle of swords, a joyful flower-battle for the sake of sport. BCA 10.9

3.36 पक्षिभ्यः सर्ववृक्षेभ्यो रश्मिभ्यो गगनादपि।
धर्मध्वनिरविश्रामं श्रूयतां सर्वदेहिभिः ॥ BCA 10.37

paksibhyah sarvavriksebhyo rasmibhyo gaganadapi
dharmadhvaniravisramam sruyatam sarvadehibhih
—BCA 10.37

Simple meaning—By means of all birds and trees, and even by rays from the sky, may the sound of Dharma be heard unceasingly by all beings. BCA 10.37

3.37 देवो वर्षतु कालेन सस्यसम्पत्तिरस्तु च।
स्फीतो भवतु लोकश्च राजा भवतु धार्मिकः ॥ BCA 10.39

devo varsatu kalena sasyasampattirastu ca
sphito bhavatu lokasca raja bhavatu dharmikah
—BCA 10.39

Simple meaning—May the god send rain in due season, and the grain be abundant, and the earth be rich, and the king rule according to Dharma. BCA 10.39

3.38 मा कश्चिद् दुःखितः सत्त्वो मा पापी मा च रोगितः।
मा हीनः परिभूतो वा मा भूतकश्चिच्च दुर्मनाः ॥ BCA 10.41

ma kascid duhkhitah sattvo ma papi ma ca rogitah
ma hinah paribhuto va ma bhutakascicca durmanah
—BCA 10.41

Simple meaning—May no being whosoever be unhappy, sinful, sick, forsaken, or despised, and none whosoever feel depressed or melancholy. BCA 10.41

Budhisattva-based ideal

3.39 For this sub-message, it is, in a way, not necessary to present any selections, because Bodhisattva is the foundation of all the Mahayana texts. This is stated in Chapter 3 of the Lotus Sutra:

इमामेवानुत्तरां सम्यक्सम्बोधिमारभ्य सर्वधर्मदेशनाभिः
बोधिसत्त्वयानमेव समादापयति ।। LS Chapter 3

imamevanuttaram samyaksambodhimarabhya
sarvadharmadesanabhih bodhisattvayanameva
samadapayati —*LS Chapter 3*

Simple meaning—All the preachings of the Lord have no other end but supreme and perfect enlightenment, for which the ideal is the Bodhisattva. LS Chapter 3

3.40 The same idea is repeatedly expressed in Bodhicaryavatara, for example, the first chapter says:-

क्षणसंपदियं सुदुर्लभा
प्रतिलब्धा पुरुषार्थसाधनी।
यदि नात्र विचिन्त्यते हितम्
पुनरप्येषः समागमः कुतः ।। BCA 1.4

ksanasampadiyam sudurlabha
pratilabdha purusarthasadhani
yadi natra vicintyate hitam
punarapyesah samagamah kutah —*BCA 1.4*

Simple meaning—This favorable moment, so hard to obtain, has arrived, leading to the achievement of men's well-being. If it is not utilized advantageously now, will the opportunity ever come again? BCA 1.4

भवदुःखशतानि तर्तुकामैः
अपि सत्त्वव्यसनानि हर्तुकामैः।

बहुसौख्यशतानि भोक्तुकामैः
न विमोच्यं हि सदैव बोधिचित्तम् ।। BCA 1.8

bhavaduhkhasatani tartukamaih
api sattvavyasanani hartukamaih
bahusaukhyasatani bhoktukamaih
na vimocyam hi sadaiva bodhicittam —*BCA 1.8*

Simple meaning—Never is the thought of Enlightenment to be relinquished by those who are desirous of escaping the hundreds of sources of existence, by those who are desirous of taking upon themselves the suffering of beings, or by those who are desirous of enjoying hundreds of pleasures. BCA 1.8

Spiritual as well as secular: Selections from Lotus Sutra.

3.41 उपायकौशल्यमनन्तु तेषाम्
भविष्यति लोकविनायकानाम्।
येना विनेष्यन्तीह प्राणकोट्यो
बौद्धस्मि ज्ञानस्मि अनास्रवस्मिन् ।। LS 2.99

upayakausalyamanantu tesam
bhavisyati lokavinayakanam
yena vinesyantiha pranakotyo
bauddhasmi jnanasmi anasravasmin —*LS 2.99*

Simple meaning—Endless will be the skilfulness of these leaders of the world, by which they will educate innumerable beings to that Buddha-knowledge which will be spiritually perfect. LS 2.99

3.42 तच्च वरिष्ठं सुमनोरमं च
विशिष्टरूपं इह सर्वलोके।
बुद्धान ज्ञानं द्विपदोत्तमानम्
उदाररूपं तद् वन्दनीयम्।। LS 3.92

tacca varistham sumanoramam ca
visistarupam iha sarvaloke
buddhana jnanam dvipadottamanam
udararupam tad vandaniyam —*LS 3.92*

Simple meaning—It is excellent and sweetest, the most exalted in the world, that knowledge of the Buddhas, the most spiritual among all knowledges, it is something sublime and adorable. LS 3.92

3.43 सुदुष्करं कुर्वति लोकनाथो
उपायकौशल्य प्रकाशयन्तः ।
हीनादिमुक्तान् दमयन्तु पुत्रान्
दमेत्व च ज्ञानमिदं ददाति ।। LS 4.49
यच्छीलमस्माभि च दीर्घरात्रम्
संरक्षितं लोकविदुस्य शासने ।
अस्माभि लब्धं फलमद्य तस्य
शीलस्य पूर्वं चरितस्य नाथ ।। LS 4.51
अद्यो वयं श्रावकभूत नाथ
संश्रावयिष्यामथ चाग्रबोधिम् ।। LS 4.53

suduskaram kurvati lokanatho
upayakausalya prakasayantah
hinadimuktan damayantu putran
dametva ca jnanamidam dadati —*LS 4.49*
yacchilamasmabhi ca dirgharatram
samraksitam lokavidusya sasane
asmabhi labdham phalamadya tasya
silasya purvam caritasya natha —*LS 4.51*
adyo vayam sravakabhuta natha
samsravayisyamatha cagrabodhim —*LS 4.53*

Simple meaning—It is a very difficult task which the Lord of the world is performing, a task in which he displays his skilfulness, when he tames his sons of low disposition and imparts to them spiritual knowledge. LS 4.49

As we have always observed the moral precepts under the rule of the knower of the world, we now receive the fruit of that morality which we have been practising. LS 4.51

Now, O Lord, we are true disciples, and we will proclaim supreme enlightenment everywhere. LS 4.53

3.44 अनागते चापि तथैव अध्वे
पूजेष्यति बुद्धसहस्रकोट्यः ।
सद्धर्मश्रेष्ठं च परिग्रहिष्यति
स्वकं च क्षेत्रं परिशोधयिष्यति ।। LS 8.12
देशेष्यति धर्म सदा विशारदो
उपायकौशल्यसहस्रकोटिभिः ।
बहूंश्च सत्त्वान् परिपाचयिष्यति
सर्वज्ञज्ञानस्मि अनास्रवस्मिन् ।। LS 8.13

anagate capi tathaiva adhve
pujesyati buddhasahasrakotyah
saddharmasrestham ca parigrahisyati
svakam ca ksetram parisodhayisyati —*LS 8.12*

desesyati dharma sada visarado
upayakausalyasahasrakotibhih
bahumsca sattvan paripacayisyati
sarvajnajnanasmi anasravasmin —*LS 8.13*

Simple meaning—In future also, he will likewise honor thousands of Buddhas, and acquire true knowledge of the most eminent dharmas, and ensure purity of his conduct.
LS 8.12

Always free from timidity, he will preach the Dharma with thousands of skilful devices, and bring many beings to full ripeness for the knowledge of the all-knowing that is spiritually perfect. LS 8.13

3.45 शाठ्यं च मानं तथा कूटनां च
अशेषतो उज्झीय धर्मभाणकः ।
ईर्ष्यां न कुर्यात् तथा जातु पण्डितो
य इच्छते सूत्रमिदं प्रकाशितुम् ।। LS 14.39

अवर्ण जातु न वदेय कस्यचिद्
दृष्टीविवादं च न जातु कुर्यात् ।
कौकृत्यस्थानं च न जातु कुर्यात्
न लप्स्यसे ज्ञानमनुत्तरं त्वम् ।। LS 14.40

sathyam ca manam tatha kutanam ca
asesato ujjhiya dharmabhanakah
irsyam na kuryat tatha jatu pandito
ya icchate sutramidam prakasitum —*LS 14.39*
avarna jatu na vadeya kasyacid
dristivivadam ca na jatu kuryat
kaukrityasthanam ca na jatu kuryat
na lapsyase jnanamanuttaram tvam —*LS 14.40*

Simple meaning—The wise Dharma-guru, the preacher, who wishes to expound the Lotus Sutra, must absolutely renounce falsehood, arrogance, calumny, and envy. LS 14.39

The preacher should never speak a disparaging word to anyone; he should never engage in a dispute on religious belief; even to those who suffer from shortcomings, he should never say "you will not obtain superior knowledge of Dharma." LS 14.40

3.46 सदा च सो आर्जवु मार्दवश्च
क्षान्तश्च भोति सुगतस्य पुत्रः।
धर्मं प्रकाशेत् पुनः पुनश्चेमम्
न तस्य खेदो भवति कदाचित् ।। LS 14.41
ये बोधिसत्त्वा दशसु दिशासु
सत्त्वानुकम्पाय चरन्ति लोके।
ते सर्वि शास्तार भवन्ति मह्यम्
गुरुगौरवं तेषु जनेत पण्डितः ।। LS 14.42

sada ca so arjavu mardavasca
ksantasca bhoti sugatasya putrah
dharmam prakaset punah punascemam
na tasya khedo bhavati kadacit —*LS 14.41*
ye bodhisattva dasasu disasu
sattvanukampaya caranti loke
te sarvi sastara bhavanti mahyam
gurugauravam tesu janeta panditah —*LS 14.42*

Simple meaning—The preacher is always sincere, mild, forbearing. As a true son of the Lord, he will repeatedly preach the true Dharma, without any feeling of annoyance.
LS 14.41

The preacher always keeps the bodhisattva-ideal in his mind. He always considers himself as a disciple of the bodhisattvas, who, out of compassion for all beings, keep moving in the world. He always feels that his spirituality is maintained because of respect to his gurus, the bodhisattvas. LS 14.42

3.47 स्मरित्वा बुद्धान् द्विपदानमुत्तमान्
जिनेषु नित्यं पितृसंज्ञ कुर्यात्।
अधिमानसंज्ञां च विहाय सर्वान्
न तस्य भोति तदन्तरायः ।। LS 14.43
श्रृणुत्वा धर्मं इममेवरूपम्
स रक्षितव्यस्तदा पण्डितेन ।। LS 14.44

smaritva buddhan dvipadanamuttaman
jinesu nityam pitrisanjna kuryat
adhimanasanjnam ca vihaya sarvan
na tasya bhoti tadantarayah —*LS 14.43*
srinutva dharmam imamevarupam
sa raksitavyastada panditena —*LS 14.44*

Simple meaning—The preacher always cherishes the memory of the Buddhas, the source of the true Dharma. The conviction that the Buddhas are the Fathers of mankind, will always keep the preacher free from arrogance, and will always protect him. LS 14.43
Visibly, it will appear that, since the preacher is bringing about the spiritual uplift of the people, they too are also protecting him (i.e. the preacher). LS 14.44

3.48 गृहाद् विहारं हि व्रजित्व धीरो
गच्छेत सूत्रं श्रवणाय एतत्।
गत्वा च सो तत्र श्रृणे मुहूर्तम्
प्रसन्नचित्तस्य फलं श्रृणोथ ।। LS 18.14

निषद्य चासौ परिषाय तत्र
शुक्लेन कर्मेण कृतेन तेन।
शक्रासनानां भवते स लाभी
ब्रह्मासनानां च नृपासनानाम् ।। LS 18.17

grihad viharam hi vrajitva dhiro
gaccheta sutram sravanaya etat
gatva ca so tatra srine muhurtam
prasannacittasya phalam srinotha —*LS 18.14*
nisadya casau parisaya tatra
suklena karmena kritena tena
sakrasananam bhavate sa labhi
brahmasananam ca nripasananam —*LS 18.17*

Simple meaning—If some wise man, to hear the Lotus Sutra, goes from his home to a monastery, and there does listen to the Sutra, with a placid mind–even if it were for a single moment–see what great benefit he gets from this. LS 18.14

Owing to the performance of this pious work, he will rise to great heights, for example, obtain seats of Indra, seats of Brahma, seats of kings. LS 18.17

3.49 ज्ञानावभासैर्गद्गदस्वरो बोधिसत्त्वो महासत्त्वोऽस्यां
सहायां लोकधातौ प्रज्ञायते। अन्येषु च गंगानदीवालिकासमेषु
लोकधातुषु बोधिसत्त्ववैनेयानां सत्त्वानां बोधिसत्त्वरूपेण
धर्मं देशयति। श्रावकवैनेयानां सत्त्वानां श्रावकरूपेण
धर्मं देशयति। प्रत्येकबुद्धवैनेयानां सत्त्वानां प्रत्येकबुद्धरूपेण
धर्मं देशयति। तथागतवैनेयानां सत्त्वानां तथागतरूपेण धर्मं देशयति

LS Chapter 24

jnanavabhasairgadgadasvaro bodhisattvo
mahasattvo'syam sahayam lokadhatau prajnayate.
anyesu ca ganganadivalikasamesu lokadhatusu
bodhisattvavaineyanam sattvanam bodhisattvarupena
dharmam desayati. sravakavaineyanam sattvanam
sravakarupena dharmam desayati. pratyekabuddha-
-vaineyanam sattvanam pratyekabuddharupena

dharmam desayati. tathagatavaineyanam sattvanam tathagatarupena dharmam desayati —*LS Chapter 24*

Simple meaning—So many are the manifestations of Dharmic knowledge by which Bodhisattva Mahasattva Gadgadasvara makes himself known in this world. To those who want to hear the Dharma from a Bodhisattva, Gadgadasvara appears in the form of a Bodhisattva. To those who want to hear the Dharma from a sravaka, Gadgadasvara appears in the form of a sravaka. To those who want to hear the Dharma from a pratyekabuddha, Gadgadasvara appears in the form of a pratyekabuddha. To those who want to hear the Dharma from a Tathagata, Gadgadasvara appears in the form of a Tathagata. LS Chapter 24

3.50 ये च एतयोः सत्पुरुषयोर्नामधेयं धारयिष्यन्ति
ते सर्वे नमस्करणीया भविष्यन्ति सदेवकेन
लोकेन। अस्मिन् खलु पुनः पूर्वयोगपरिवर्ते
भाष्यमाणे चतुरशीतीनां प्राणिसहस्राणां विरजो
विगतमलं धर्मेषु धर्मचक्षुर्विशुद्धम् ।। LS Chapter 27

ye ca etayoh satpurusayornamadheyam dharayisyanti te sarve namaskaraniya bhavisyanti sadevakena lokena. asmin khalu punah purvayogaparivarte bhasyamane caturasitinam pranisahasranam virajo vigatamalam dharmesu dharmacaksurvisuddham —*LS Chapter 27*

Simple meaning—The two sons of King Subhavyuha were so great, spiritually, that by cherishing their names, the aspirants will become worthy of receiving homage from all men as well as gods. While this story of the two princes was being narrated, the spiritual insight of eighty-four thousand living beings became perfectly pure. LS Chapter 27

3.51 यथापि पुरुषो भवि कश्चिदेव
प्रविष्ट स स्यादिह मित्रशालम्।
मित्रं च तस्य धनवन्तमाढ्यम्
स तस्य दद्याद् बहु खाद्यभोज्यम् ।। LS 8.36

yathapi puruso bhavi kascideva
pravista sa syadiha mitrasalam
mitram ca tasya dhanavantamadhyam
sa tasya dadyad bahu khadyabhojyam —*LS 8.36*

Simple meaning—This is a story in which a certain man goes to the house of one of his friends. This friend, being very rich, gives to the visiting man, plenty of food, of various kinds. LS 8.36

संतर्पयित्वा च तं भोजनेन
अनेकमूल्यं रत्नं च दद्यात्।
बद्ध्वान्तरीये वसनांति ग्रंथिम्
दत्वा च तस्येह भवेत तुष्टः ।। LS 8.37

santarpayitva ca tam bhojanena
anekamulyam ratnam ca dadyat
baddhvantariye vasananti granthim
datva ca tasyeha bhaveta tustah —*LS 8.37*

Simple meaning—After satiating the visiting friend with nourishment, he also gives him (secretly) a jewel of great value - he ties it with a knot within the friend's upper robe, and feels happy at having given the jewel (although he does not tell the friend about it). LS 8.37

सो चापि प्रकान्तु भवेत बालो
उत्थाय सोऽन्यं नगरं व्रजेत।
सो कृच्छ्रप्राप्तः कृपणो गवेशी
आहार पर्येषति खिद्यमानः ।। LS 8.38

so capi prakrantu bhaveta balo
utthaya so'nyam nagaram vrajeta
so kricchrapraptah kripano gavesi
ahara paryesati khidyamanah —*LS 8.38*

Simple meaning—The visiting friend, unaware of the jewel hidden in his robe, goes forth from the rich friend's home and travels to another town. There he is befallen with misfortune and, as a miserable beggar, seeks his food to remain alive. LS 8.38

पर्येषितः भोजननिर्वृतः स्याद्
भक्तं उदारं अविचिन्तयन्तः।
तं चापि रत्नं हि भवेत विस्मृतम्
बद्ध्वान्तरीये स्मृतिरस्य नास्ति ।। LS 8.39

paryesitah bhojananirvritah syad
bhaktam udaram avicintayantah
tam capi ratnam hi bhaveta vismritam
baddhvantariye smritirasya nasti —*LS 8.39*

Simple meaning—The poor friend is contended with the pittance he gets by begging, without even thinking of the dainty food that he had at his rich friend's home. As to that jewel, he has no idea–he is not at all aware that any jewel was tied in his upper robe by his rich friend. LS 8.39

तमेव सो पश्यति पूर्वमित्रो
येनास्य दत्तं रत्नं गृहे स्वे।
तमेव सुष्ठुः परिभाषयित्वा
दर्शेति रत्नं वसनान्तरस्मिन् ।। LS 8.40

tameva so pasyati purvamitro
yenasya dattam ratnam grihe sve
tameva susthuh paribhasayitva
darseti ratnam vasanantarasmin —*LS 8.40*

Simple meaning—Under these circumstances, the poor friend is seen by his rich friend (who at his home had given him that jewel). The rich friend politely reprimands him and shows him the jewel hidden in his robe. LS 8.40

दृष्ट्वा च सो परमसुखैः समर्पितो
रत्नस्य तस्य अनुभव ईदृशः।
महाधनी कोशबली च सो भवेत्
समर्पितः कामगुणेहि पंचहि ।। LS 8.41

dristva ca so paramasukhaih samarpito
ratnasya tasya anubhava idrisah
mahadhani kosabali ca so bhavet
samarpitah kamagunehi pancahi —*LS 8.41*

Simple meaning—At this sight, the poor friend feels extremely happy–the value of the jewel is such that he becomes a very rich man, of great power, and in possession of all that the five senses can enjoy. LS 8.41

3.52 स चापि प्रोत्साहितु तेन सत्त्वः
श्रूणेय सूत्रेम मुहूर्तकमपि।
तस्यापि धर्मस्य फलं श्रृणोहि
मुखरोग तस्य न कदाचि भोति ।। LS 18.10

sa capi protsahitu tena sattvah
sruneya sutrema muhurtakamapi
tasyapi dharmasya phalam srinohi
mukharoga tasya na kadaci bhoti —*LS 18.10*

Simple meaning—If a man hears, with enthusiasm, the Lotus Sutra, even for a moment, see what fruit results from that good deed. He will never have a mouth disease. LS 18.10

जिह्वापि तस्य न कदाचि दुःखति
न तस्य दन्ता पतिता भवन्ति।
श्यामाथ पीता विषमा च जातु
बीभत्सितोष्ठो न च जातु भोति ।। LS 18.11

jihvapi tasya na kadaci duhkhati
na tasya danta patita bhavanti
syamatha pita visama ca jatu
bibhatsitostho na ca jatu bhoti —*LS 18.11*

Simple meaning—His tongue will never be sore, his teeth will never fall out, never be black, yellow, unequal; his lips will never become loathsome. LS 18.11

कुटिलं च सूक्षं च न जातु दीर्घम्
मुखं न चिपितं स्य कदाचि भोति।
सुसंस्थिता नास तथा ललाटम्
दन्ता च ओष्ठो मुखमण्डलं च ।। LS 18.12

kutilam ca suksam ca na jatu dirgham
mukham na cipitam sya kadachi bhoti

susamsthita nasa tatha lalatam
danta ca ostho mukhamandalam ca —*LS 18.12*

Simple meaning—His face will never be wry, nor lean, nor long, his nose will never be flat; similarly, his forehead, teeth, and lips, will all be well-formed. LS 18.12

प्रियदर्शनो भोति सदा नराणाम्
पूर्तिं च वक्रं न कदापि भोति।
यथोत्पलस्येह सदा सुगंधिः
प्रवायते तस्य मुखस्य गंधः ।। LS 18.13

priyadarsano bhoti sada naranam
purtim ca vakram na kadapi bhoti
yathotpalasyeha sada sugandhih
pravayate tasya mukhasya gandhah —*LS 18.13*

Simple meaning—His personality will always be pleasant to men, his breath will be sweet-smelling like lotus, and his companionship will give pleasure to all. LS 18.13

सुगौरु तस्य भवत्यात्मभावः
परियाति सो अश्वरथेहि धीरः।
हस्तीरथांश्च अभिरुह्य उच्चान्
रत्नेहि चित्राननुचंक्रमेया ।। LS 18.15

sugauru tasya bhavatyatmabhavah
pariyati so asvarathehi dhirah
hastirathamsca abhiruhya uccan
ratnehi citrananucankrameya —*LS 18.15*

Simple meaning—His appearance will be attractive, he will be driven in horse-carriages, like wise men, or mounted on elevated carriages drawn by elephants, and decorated with gems. LS 18.15

विभूषितां सो शिबिकां लभेत
नरैरनेकैरिह वाह्यमानाम्।
गत्वापि धर्मं श्रवणाय तस्य
फलं शुभं भोति च एवरूपम् ।। LS 18.16

vibhusitam so sibikam labheta
narairanekairiha vahyamanan
gatvapi dharmam sravanaya tasya
phalam subham bhoti ca evarupam —*LS 18.16*

Simple meaning—He will be honored with ornaments and carried by numerous men respectfully. Such is the remarkable fruit of his going to hear the preaching of the Lotus Sutra. LS 18.16

3.53 अथ खलु भगवान् सततसमिताभियुक्तं बोधिसत्त्वं महासत्त्वमामन्त्रयामास। यः कश्चित् कुलपुत्र इमं धर्मपर्यायं धारयिष्यति वाचयिष्यति वा देशयिष्यति वा लिखिष्यति वा स कुलपुत्रो वा कुलदुहिता वा अष्टौ चक्षुर्गुणशतानि प्रतिलप्स्यते द्वादश श्रोत्रगुणशतानि प्रतिलप्स्यते अष्टौ कायगुणशतानि प्रतिलप्स्यते द्वादश जिह्वागुणशतानि प्रतिलप्स्यते अष्टौ घ्राणगुणशतानि प्रतिलप्स्यते द्वादश मनोगुणशतानि प्रतिलप्स्यते तस्यैभिर्बहुभिर्गुणशतैः षडिंद्रियग्रामः परिशुद्धः सुपरिशुद्धो भविष्यति ।।

LS Chapter 19

atha khalu bhagavan satatasamitabhiyuktam bodhisattvam mahasattvamamantrayamasa. yah kascit kulaputra imam dharmaparyayam dharayisyati vacayisyati va desayisyati va likhisyati va sa kulaputro va kuladuhita va astau caksurgunasatani pratilapsyate dvadasa srotragunasatani pratilapsyate astau kayagunasatani pratilapsyate dvadasa jihvagunasatani pratilapsyate astau ghranagunasatani pratilapsyate dvadasa manogunasatani pratilapsyate tasyaibhirbahubhirgunasataih sadindriyagramah parisuddhah suparisuddho bhavisyati.

—*LS Chapter 19*

Simple meaning—The Lord then addressed the Bodhisattva Mahasattva Satatasamitabhiyukta (i.e. ever and constantly strenuous). Any one, young man of good family, who shall keep, teach, write the Lotus Sutra, or have it written, let that person be a young man of good family or a young lady, will obtain eight hundred good qualities of the eye, twelve hundred of the ear, eight hundred of the nose, twelve hundred of the tongue, eight hundred of the body, twelve hundred of the mind. By these many hundred good qualities, the whole of the six organs shall be perfect, thoroughly perfect. LS Chapter 19

3.54 तडाग इव तृषितानामग्निरिव शीतार्तानां चैलमिव
नग्नानां सार्थवाह इव वणिजानां मातेव पुत्राणां नौरिव
पारगामिनां वैद्य इव आतुराणां दीप इव
तमोन्धकारावृतानां रत्नमिव धनार्थिनां चक्रवर्तीव
सर्वकोट्टराजानां समुद्र इव सरितामुल्केव
सर्वतमोन्धकारविधमनाय। एवमेव नक्षत्रराजसंकुसुमिताभिज्ञ
अयं सद्धर्मपुण्डरीको धर्मपर्याय: सर्वदु:खप्रमोचक:
सर्वव्याधिच्छेदक: सर्वसंसारभयबंधनसंकटप्रमोचक: ।। LS Chapter 23

tadaga iva trisitanamagniriva sitartanam cailamiva nagnanam sarthavaha iva vanijanam mateva putranam nauriva paragaminam vaidya iva aturanam dipa iva tamondhakaravritanam ratnamiva dhanarthinam cakravartiva sarvakottarajanam samudra iva saritamulkeva sarvatamondhakaravidhamanaya. evameva naksatrarajasankusumitabhijna ayam saddharmapundariko dharmaparyayah sarvaduhkhapramocakah sarvavyadhicchedakah sarvasamsarabhayabandhanasankatapramocakah.

—LS Chapter 23

Simple meaning—The Dharma of this Lotus Sutra is like a tank for the thirsty, like a fire for those who suffer from cold, like a garment for the naked, like the caravan leader for the merchants, like a mother for her children, like a boat for those who want to go to the other shore, like a physician for the sick, like a lamp for those who are wrapt in darkness, like a jewel for those who want wealth, like the ocean for the rivers, like a torch for the dispelling of darkness. So, Naksatrarajasamkusumitabhijna, this Dharma of the Lotus Sutra delivers from all evils, cures all diseases, releases from the narrow bonds of samsara. LS Chapter 23

Spiritual as well as secular: Selections from Bodhicaryavatara

3.55 पूज्यन्तां सर्वसम्बुद्धाः सर्वसत्त्वैरनेकधा।
अचिन्त्यबौद्धसौख्येन सुखिनः सन्तु भूयसा ।। BCA 10.48

pujyantam sarvasambuddhah sarvasattvairanekadha
acintyabauddhasaukhyena sukhinah santu bhuyasa
—BCA 10.48

Simple meaning—May all the Buddhas be worshipped in all ways by all beings. May the worshippers too attain the happiness of Enlightenment. BCA 10.48

3.56 अभुक्त्वापायिकं दुःखं विना दुष्करचर्यया।
दिव्येनैकेन कायेन जगद् बुद्धत्वमाप्नुयात् ।। BCA 10.47
abhuktvapayikam duhkham vina duskaracaryaya
divyenaikena kayena jagad buddhatvamapnuyat
—BCA 10.47

Simple meaning—Without suffering the sorrow of worldly problems, and without painful experiences, may all living beings obtain the supreme state of Buddhahood by means of physical and mental discipline. BCA 10.47

3.57 सिध्यन्तु बोधिसत्त्वानां जगदर्थं मनोरथाः।
यच्चिन्तयन्ति ते नाथाः तत्सत्त्वानां समृध्यतु ।। BCA 10.49
sidhyantu bodhisattvanam jagadartham manorathah
yaccintayanti te nathah tatsattvanam samridhyatu
—BCA 10.49

Simple meaning—May that which has been desired by the Bodhisattvas for the benefit of the world, succeed. Whatever those Enlightened well-wishers want, may that be accomplished by human beings. BCA 10.49

3.58 प्रत्येकबुद्धाः सुखिनो भवन्तु श्रावकास्तथा।
देवासुरनरैर्नित्यं पूज्यमानाः सगौरवैः ।। BCA 10.50
pratyekabuddhah sukhino bhavantu sravakastatha
devasuranarairnityam pujyamanah sagauravaih
—BCA 10.50

Simple meaning—In the same way, may Pratyekabuddhas and Sravakas be happy, and may they always receive honor and worship, from devas, asuras, and human beings. BCA 10.50

3.59 पाठस्वाध्याय कलिला विहाराः सन्तु सुस्थिताः ।
नित्यं स्यात् संघसामग्री संघकार्यं च सिध्यतु ॥ BCA 10.42

pathasvadhyayakalila viharah santu susthitah
nityam syat sanghasamagri sanghakaryam ca sidhyatu

—BCA 10.42

Simple meaning—May the monasteries continue their spiritual activities peacefully and smoothly, maintaining the highest standard in regard to study, research and recitation. May the sanghas be well-equipped, to carry on their work successfully. BCA 10.42

3.60 विवेकलाभिनः सन्तु शिक्षाकामाश्च भिक्षवः ॥
कर्मण्यचित्ता ध्यायन्तु सर्वविक्षेपवर्जिताः ॥ BCA 10.43

vivekalabhinah santu siksakamasca bhiksavah
karmanyacitta dhyayantu sarvaviksepavarjitah

—BCA 10.43

Simple meaning—May the monks maintain successfully, their discrimination and zeal for the disciplined lifestyle. May they meditate with deep concentration, free from all distraction.

BCA 10.43

3.61 लाभिन्यः सन्तु भिक्षुण्यः कलहायासवर्जिताः ।
भवन्त्वखण्डशीलाश्च सर्वे प्रव्रजितास्तथा ॥ BCA 10.44

labhinyah santu bhiksunyah kalahayasavarjitah
bhavantvakhandasilasca sarve pravrajitastatha

—BCA 10.44

Simple meaning—May the nuns receive the same honor as the monks, free from discrimination and prejudice. May their practice of self–discipline continue without hindrance.

BCA 10.44

3.62 वस्त्रभोजनपानीयं स्रक्चन्दनविभूषणम् ।
मनोभिलषितं सर्वं लभन्तां हितसंहितम् ॥ BCA 10.20

vastrabhojanapaniyam srakcandanavibhusanam
manobhilasitam sarvam labhantam hitasamhitam

—BCA 10.20

Simple meaning—May all the people have clothes, food and drink, garlands, sandalwood fragrance, ornaments, in fact, all that their hearts desire and all that they think is beneficial to them. BCA 10.20

3.63 क्षुत्पिपासाव्यथां हन्यामन्नपानप्रवर्षणैः ।
दुर्भिक्षान्तरकल्पेषु भवेयं पानभोजनम् ।। BCA 3.8
ksutpipasavyatham hanyamannapanapravarsanaih
durbhiksantarakalpesu bhaveyam panabhojanam
—*BCA 3.8*

Simple meaning—With rains of food and drink, may I dispel the anguish of hunger and thirst. At the time of a devastating famine, may I be able to supply food and drink. BCA 3.8

3.64 आरोग्यं रोगिणामस्तु मुच्यन्तां सर्वबंधनात् ।
दुर्बला बलिनः सन्तु स्निग्धचित्ताः परस्परम् ।। BCA 10.22
arogyam roginamastu mucyantam sarvabandhanat
durbala balinah santu snigdhacittah parasparam
—*BCA 10.22*

Simple meaning—May the sick be well, may all be freed from bondage; may the weak become strong. Above all, may mutually affectionate thoughts prevail. BCA 10.22

3.65 ग्लानानामस्मि भैषज्यं भवेयं वैद्य एव च ।
तदुपस्थायकश्चैव यावद्रोगापुनर्भवः ।। BCA 3.7
glananamasmi bhaisajyam bhaveyam vaidya eva ca
tadupasthayakascaiva yavadrogapunarbhavah
—*BCA 3.7*

Simple meaning—I want to provide medicine for the sick. May I be their physician as well as their servant, until sickness is completely gone (and does not come back). BCA 3.7

3.66 सर्वा दिशाः शिवाः सन्तु सर्वेषां पथिवर्तिनाम् ।
येन कार्येण गच्छन्ति तदुपायेन सिध्यतु ।। BCA 10.23

sarva disah sivah santu sarvesam pathivartinam
yena karyena gacchanti tadupayena sidhyatu
—*BCA 10.23*

Simple meaning—May all regions be safe and auspicious for those who travel by road. May every effort succeed which will help people achieve their goals. BCA 10.23

3.67 नौयानयात्रारूढाश्च सन्तु सिद्धमनारेथाः ।
क्षेमेण कूलमासाद्य रमन्तां सहबन्धुभिः ।। BCA 10.24

nauyanayatrarudhasca santu siddhamanorathah
ksemena kulamasadya ramantam sahabandhubhih
—*BCA 10.24*

Simple meaning—May those experiencing difficulty in their sea voyage, find fulfilment of their heart's desire. Having peacefully arrived at their destination, may they rejoice with their relatives and friends. BCA 10.24

3.68 कान्तारोन्मार्गपतिता लभन्तां सार्थसंगतिम् ।
अश्रमेण च गच्छन्तु चौरव्याघ्रादिनिर्भयाः ।। BCA 10.25

kantaronmargapatita labhantam sarthasangatim
asramena ca gacchantu cauravyaghradinirbhayah
—*BCA 10.25*

Simple meaning—May those who are walking through a trackless, uninhabited area, find a friendly caravan, and may they travel without fatigue and without fear from robbers, tigers, etc. BCA 10.25

3.69 दरिद्राणां च सत्त्वानां निधिः स्यामहमक्षयः ।
नानोपकरणाकारैरुपतिष्ठेयमग्रतः ।। BCA 3.9

daridranam ca sattvanam nidhih syamahamaksayah
nanopakaranakarairupatistheyamagratah —*BCA 3.9*

Simple meaning—To help the needy, poor people, may I be able to provide assistance without any limit. May they know that I want to do whatever is beneficial to them in every possible way. (BCA 3.9)

3.70 अनाथानामहं नाथः सार्थवाहश्च यायिनाम्।
पारेप्सुनां च नौभूतः सेतुः संक्रम एव च ।। BCA 3.17

anathanamaham nathah sarthavahasca yayinam
parepsunam ca naubhutah setuh sankrama eva ca
—BCA 3.17

Simple meaning—I want to be a protector for those who have no protection, a companion for those who would like to travel (but have no company), and a boat, a bridge, a passage for those who would like to reach the other shore. BCA 3.17

3.71 दीपार्थिनामहं दीपः शय्या शय्यार्थिनामहम्।
दासार्थिनामहं दासो भवेयं सर्वदेहिनाम् ।। BCA 3.18

diparthinamaham dipah sayya sayyarthinamaham
dasarthinamaham daso bhaveyam sarvadehinam
—BCA 3.18

Simple meaning—I want to be a lantern for those who have no lantern, I want to be a bed for those who have no bed to sleep on, I want to be a helper for those who need help – in other words, I want to help all poor and needy people. BCA 3.18

3.72 चिंतामणिर्भद्रघटः सिद्धविद्या महौषधिः।
भवेयं कल्पवृक्षश्च कामधेनुश्च देहिनाम् ।। BCA 3.19

cintamanirbhadraghatah siddhavidya mahausadhih
bhaveyam kalpavriksasca kamadhenusca dehinam
—BCA 3.19

Simple meaning—To satisfy the needs of people, I would like to be a magic jewel, an inexhaustible jar, a powerful spell, an unfailing medicine, a wish-fulfilling tree, a wish-fulfilling cow. BCA 3.19

3.73 पण्डिताः संस्कृताः सन्तु लाभिनः पिण्डपातिकाः।
भवन्तु शुद्धसन्तानाः सर्वदिक् ख्यातिकीर्तयः ।। BCA 10.46

panditah sanskritah santu labhinah pindapatikah
bhavantu suddhasantanah sarvadik khyatikirtayah
—BCA 10.46

Simple meaning—May scholars be honored, well-received and given awards. May the next generation of scholars be assured that they too will be similarly honored. BCA 10.46

3.74 शर्करादिव्यपेता च समा पाणितलोपमा।
मृद्वी च वैडूर्यमयी भूमिः सर्वत्र तिष्ठतु ।। BCA 10.35

sarkaradivyapeta ca sama panitalopama
mridvi ca vaiduryamayi bhumih sarvatra tisthatu
—BCA 10.35

Simple meaning—May the surface of the earth be smooth – such that human beings can put it to good use. Let the interior of the earth contain useful minerals and jewels. BCA 10.35

3.75 पृथिव्यादीनि भूतानि निःशेषाकाशवासिनाम्।
सत्त्वानामप्रेयाणां यथाभोगान्यनेकधा ।। BCA 3.20
एवं आकाशनिष्ठस्य सत्त्वधातोरनेकधा।
भवेयमुपजीव्योऽहं यावत् सर्वे न निर्वृताः ।। BCA 3.21

prithivyadini bhutani nihsesakasavasinam
sattvanamapreyanam yathabhoganyanekadha
—BCA 3.20

evam akasanisthasya sattvadhatoranekadha
bhaveyamupajivyoham yavat sarve na nirvritah
—BCA 3.21

Simple meaning—Just as the earth and other natural elements are, in various ways, for the enjoyment of innumerable beings, dwelling in all of space, similarly I want to be, in various ways, the means of sustenance for the living beings occupying space, for as long as such need remains. BCA 3.20-21

No discrimination : Selections from Lotus Sutra.

3.76 स्वरेण चैकेन वदामि धर्मं
बोधिं निदानं करियाण नित्यम्।

समं हि एतद् विषमत्व नास्ति
न कश्चि विद्वेषु न रागु विद्यते ।। LS 5.21

svarena caikena vadami dharmam
bodhim nidanam kariyana nityam
samam hi etad visamatva nasti
na kaschi vidvesu na ragu vidyate —*LS 5.21*

Simple meaning—I preach always with the same voice, constantly taking enlightenment as my text. My preaching is the same for all, there is no partiality in it; similarly, there is neither hatred nor attachment. LS 5.21

3.77 अनुनीयता मह्य न काचिदस्ति
प्रेमा च दोषश्च न मे कहिंचित्।
समं च धर्मं प्रवदामि देहिनाम्
यथैकसत्त्वस्य तथा परस्य ।। LS 5.22

anuniyata mahya na kacidasti
prema ca dosasca na me kahincit
samam ca dharmam pravadami dehinam
yathaikasattvasya tatha parasya —*LS 5.22*

Simple meaning—I am impartial; have no attachment nor hatred towards any one. I proclaim the same Dharma to all beings, without distinction, that is, to the one as to the other. LS 5.22

3.78 संतर्पयामि इमु सर्वलोकं
मेघो व वारिं सम मुंचमानः।
आर्येषु नीचेषु च तुल्यबुद्धिः
दुःशीलभूतेष्वथ शीलवत्सु ।। LS 5.24

santarpayami imu sarvalokam
megho va varim sama muncamanah
aryesu nicesu ca tulyabuddhih
duhsilabhutesvatha silavatsu —*LS 5.24*

Simple meaning—I look after the whole world like a cloud shedding its water without distinction. I have the same approach to respectable people as to the low, to moral persons as to the immoral. LS 5.24

3.79 विनष्टचारित्र तथैव ये नरा:
चारित्राचारसमन्विताश्च।
दृष्टिस्थिता ये च विनष्टदृष्टि
सम्यग्दृशो ये चाविशुद्धदृष्टय: ।। LS 5.25

vinastacaritra tathaiva ye narah
caritracarasamanvitasca
drististhita ye ca vinastadristi
samyagdriso ye cavisuddhadristayah —LS 5.25

Simple meaning—I am the same for all—for the depraved as for those who observe the rules of good conduct; for those who hold sectarian views and unsound tenets, as for those whose views are sound and correct. LS 5.25

3.80 हीनेषु चोत्कृष्टमतीषु चापि
मृद्विन्द्रियेषु प्रवदामि धर्मम्।
किलासितां सर्व विवर्जयित्वा
सम्यक् प्रमुंचाम्यहु धर्मवर्षम् ।। LS 5.26

hinesu cotkristamatisu capi
mridvindriyesu pravadami dharmam
kilasitam sarva vivarjayitva
samyak pramuncamyahu dharmavarsam —LS 5.26

Simple meaning—I preach the Dharma to the so-called inferior as well as to persons of superior understanding and extraordinary faculties. Unaffected by constant preaching, I spread everywhere, and for all, the rain of the Dharma. LS 5.26

3.81 अस्ति कुलपुत्र सागरस्य नागराज्ञो दुहिता अष्टवर्षा जात्या
महाप्रज्ञा तीक्ष्णेन्द्रिया ज्ञानपूर्वंगमेन कायवाङ्‌मनस्कर्मणा
समन्वागता सर्वतथागतभाषितव्यंजनार्थोद्ग्रहणे
धारणीप्रतिलब्धा सर्वधर्मसत्त्वसमाधानसमाधिसहस्रैक-
-क्षणप्रतिलाभिनी। बोधिचित्ताविनिवर्तिनी

विस्तीर्णप्रणिधाना सर्वसत्त्वेषु आत्मप्रेमानुगता गुणोत्पादने
च समर्था। न च तेभ्यः परिहीयते। स्मितमुखी
परमया शुभवर्णपुष्कलतया समन्वागता मैत्रचित्ता
करुणां च वाचं भाषते। सा सम्यक्सम्बोधिं
अभिसम्बोद्धुं समर्था ।। LS Chapter 12

asti kulaputra sagarasya nagarajno duhita astavarsa jatya mahaprajna tiksnendriya jnanapurvamgamena kayavanmanaskarmana samanvagata sarvatathagatabhasitavyanjana--rthodgrahane dharanipratilabdha sarvadharmasattvasamadhanasamadhisahasraika--ksanapratilabhini bodhicittavinivartini vistirnapranidhana sarvasattvesu atmapremanugata gunotpadane ca samartha na ca tebhyah parihiyate smitamukhi paramaya subhavarnapuskalataya samanvagata maitracitta karunam ca vacam bhasate sa samyaksambodhim abhisamboddhum samartha

—*LS Chapter 12*

Simple meaning—O young man of good family, there is the daughter of Sagara, the Naga-king, eight year old, very intelligent, of keen faculties, endowed with prudence in actions of body, speech, and mind, who has understood and preserved all the teachings, in substance and form, of the Tathagatas, who has acquired in one moment a thousand meditations and proofs of the essence of true Dharma. She does not swerve from the idea of enlightenment, has great aspirations, applies to other beings the same measure as to herself, she is apt to display all virtues, and is never deficient in them. With a pleasing smile on her face and in the bloom of an extremely handsome appearance, she speaks words of kindliness and compassion. She is fit to arrive at supreme, perfect enlightenment. LS Chapter 12

3.82 ये चापि सत्त्वा इह लोकधातौ
अभ्यन्तरे बाहिरि ये वसन्ति।
देवा मनुष्यासुरगुह्यकाश्च
नागाश्च ये चापि तिरश्च योनिषु ।। LS 19.69

षट्सु गतिषु निवसन्ति सत्त्वा
विचिन्तितं तेष भवेत यं च।
एकक्षणे सर्वि विदुर्विजानते
धारेत्व सूत्रं इम आनुशंसाः ।। LS 19.70

ye capi sattva iha lokadhatau
abhyantare bahiri ye vasanti
deva manusyasuraguhyakasca
nagasca ye capi tirasca yonisu *—LS 19.69*
satsu gatisu nivasanti sattva
vicintitam tesa bhaveta yam ca
ekaksane sarvi vidurvijanate
dharetva sutram ima anusamsah *—LS 19.70*

Simple meaning—For the sage, all are equal, for example, beings living in this world, within or without, gods, men, demons, goblins, Nagas, brutes; LS 19.69

beings stationed in any of the six conditions of existence. All their thoughts, the sage knows instantaneously. These are the advantages of keeping the Lotus Sutra. LS 19.70

3.83 तस्य जिनस्य परिनिवृतस्य
सद्धर्म संक्षोभ व्रजन्ति पश्चिमे।
भिक्षु अभूषी तद बोधिसत्त्वो
नामेन सो सदापरिभूत उच्यते ।। LS 20.2

tasya jinasya parinivritasya
saddharma samksobha vrajanti pascime
bhiksu abhusi tada bodhisattvo
namena so sadaparibhuta ucyate *—LS 20.2*

Simple meaning—At that time, succeeding that Buddha, when the decay of the true Dharma was far advanced, there was a monk, a Boddhisattva, called by the name of Sadaparibhuta (to whom all were equal). LS 20.2

उपसंक्रमित्वा तद भिक्षु अन्यान्
उपलम्भदृष्टिना तथैव भिक्षुणी।

परिभाव मह्यं न कदाचिदस्ति
यूयं हि चर्यां चरथाग्रबोधये ।। LS 20.3

upasamkramitva tada bhiksu anyan
upalambhadristina tathaiva bhiksuni
paribhava mahyam na kadacidasti
yuyam hi caryam carathagrabodhaye —*LS 20.3*

Simple meaning—Sadaparibhuta would approach and say to every one, "I do not criticize you nor condemn you, because you are following the course leading to supreme enlightenment." All the monks and nuns saw this, but it was so hard for them to believe in Sadaparibhuta's words. LS 20.3

एवं च संश्रावयि नित्यकालम्
आक्रोश परिभाष सहन्तु तेषाम् ।। LS 20.4

evam ca samsravayi nityakalam
akrosa paribhasa sahantu tesam —*LS 20.4*

Simple meaning—Since people did not believe in Sadaparibhuta's words, they abused him. But Sadaparibhuta tolerated all abuse and kept on addressing every one, without distinction, as before. LS 20.4

3.84 ये चापि सर्वे बहु ओपलम्भिका
बोधीय तेन परिपाचितासीत्।
ततश्च्यवित्वान स बोधिसत्त्वो
आरागयी बुद्धसहस्रकोट्यः ।। LS 20.6

ye capi sarve bahu opalambhika
bodhiya tena paripacitasit
tatascyavitvana sa bodhisattvo
aragayi buddhasahasrakotyah —*LS 20.6*

Simple meaning—Since Sadaparibhuta had the blessings of all the Buddhas, his words proved to be true. Even those people, who thought themselves to be unfit, did attain enlightenment. LS 20.6

3.85 अनुपूर्व पुण्येन कृतेन तेन
प्रकाशयित्वा इमु सूत्र नित्यम्।
बोधिं स सम्प्राप्त जिनस्य पुत्रो
अहमेव सो शाक्यमुनिस्तदासीत् ।। LS 20.7

anupurva punyena kritena tena
prakasayitva imu sutra nityam
bodhim sa samparapta jinasya putro
ahameva so sakyamunistadasit —*LS 20.7*

Simple meaning—Sakyamuni Buddha said, "This Bodhisattva (Sadaparibhuta) performed so many good deeds (because of him so many people attained enlightenment), and he constantly promulgated the Lotus Sutra. No wonder, because it was I in the form of Sadaparibhuta." LS 20.7

3.86 अयमेव स पद्मश्रीबोधिसत्त्वो महासत्त्वः तेन
कालेन तेन समयेन शुभव्यूहो नाम राजाभूत्।
स्यात् खलु पुनः कुलपुत्रा युष्माकं कांक्षा वा
विमतिर्वा विचिकित्सा वान्या सा तेन कालेन
तेन समयेन विमलदत्ता नाम राजभार्याभूत्। न खलु
पुनः कुलपुत्रा युष्माभिरेवं द्रष्टव्यम्। तत्कस्य हेतोः।
अयं स वैरोचनरश्मिप्रतिमण्डितध्वजराजो नाम
बोधिसत्त्वो महासत्त्वस्तेन कालेन तेन समयेन विमलदत्ता
नाम राजभार्याभूत्। तस्य राज्ञः शुभव्यूहस्यानुकम्पायै
तेषां च सत्त्वानां राज्ञः शुभव्यूहस्य
भार्यात्वमभ्युपगतोऽभूत्।। LS Chapter 27

ayameva sa padmasribodhisattvo mahasattvah tena
kalena tena samayena subhavyuho nama rajabhut
syat khalu punah kulaputra yusmakam kamksa va
vimatirva vicikitsa vanya sa ten kalena
tena samayena vimaladatta nama rajabharyabhut na
khalu punah kulaputra yusmabhirevam drastavyam
tatkasya hetoh ayam sa vairocanarasmipratimandita-
-dhvajarajo nama bodhisattvo mahasattvastena kalena
tena samayena vimaladatta nama rajabharyabhut

tasya rajnah subhavyuhasyanukampayai tesam ca sattvanam rajnah subhavyuhasya bharyatvam-abhyupagatobhut *—LS Chapter 27*

Simple meaning—It is the same Bodhisattva Mahasattva Padmasri (who is present here now), who at that time was king Subhavyuha. O young men of good family, you might have some curiosity as to who was queen Vimaladatta at that time. So I want to clarify that. It was another Bodhisattva Mahasattva called Vairocanarasmipratimanditadhvajaraja who, at that time, was queen Vimaladatta—in fact, this Bodhisattva, out of compassion for king Subhavyuha, had taken the form of his wife i.e. queen Vimaladatta. LS Chapter 27

No Discrimination : Selections from Bodhicaryavatara.

3.87 बोधिचित्तं समुत्पाद्य सर्वसत्त्वसुखेच्छया।
त्रैलोक्यपूज्यं बुद्धत्वं सत्त्वानां किल वांछसि।। BCA 6.80-81

bodhicittam samutpadya sarvasattvasukhecchaya
trailokyapujyam buddhatvam sattvanam kila vamchasi
—BCA 6.80-81

Simple meaning—Once you cultivate the thought of enlightenment, you always desire that all the beings–without any exception–should be happy. Such universality arises automatically when Buddhahood is your goal. BCA 6.80-81

3.88 अनेन मम पुण्येन सर्वसत्त्वा अशेषतः।
विरम्य सर्वपापेभ्यः कुर्वन्तु कुशलं सदा ।। BCA 10.31
बोधिचित्ताविरहिता बोधिचर्यापरायणाः।
बुद्धैः परिगृहीताश्च मारकर्मविवर्जिताः ।। BCA 10.32

anena mama punyena sarvasattva asesatah
viramya sarvapapebhyah kurvantu kusalam sada
—BCA 10.31

bodhicittavirahita bodhicaryaparayanah
buddhaih parigrihitasca marakarmavivarjitah
—BCA 10.32

Simple meaning—Whatever merit I have acquired, I want that to bring about improvement in the lives of all the people, without any exception. May they stay away from all evils, and help one another in doing good deeds. May they never be separated from the thought of enlightenment. May they remain devoted to the way of enlightenment, protected by the Buddhas so that Mara can not exert any negative influence. BCA 3.31-32

3.89 दशदिग्व्योमपर्यन्तसर्वसत्त्वार्थसाधने।
यथा चरति मंजुश्री सैव चर्या भवेन्मम।। BCA 10.54

dasadigvyomaparyantasarvasattvarthasadhane
yatha carati manjusri saiva carya bhavenmama
—BCA 10.54

Simple meaning—In strenghening my desire to avoid discrimination completely, I draw inspiration from Manjusri-just as Manjusri constantly moves all over the world and the skies, to bring about happiness and prosperity of all beings, let me do the same, in accordance with my limited capability. BCA 10.54

3.90 सर्वेऽपि वैद्याः कुर्वन्ति क्रियादुःखैररोगताम् ।। BCA 7.23
गर्भिण्यश्च प्रसूयन्तां मायादेवीव निर्व्यथाः ।। BCA 10.19

sarve'pi vaidyah kurvanti kriyaduhkhairarogatam
—BCA 7.23

garbhinyasca prasuyantam mayadeviva nirvyathah
—BCA 10.19

Simple meaning—All physicians look after the health of people, without any discrimination. May pregnant women receive all medical help and deliver healthy babies, safely, recalling how queen Maya gave birth to the Buddha. (Although Queen Maya died a week after the birth of the Buddha, modern women's death at childbirth has to be avoided with medical help). BCA 7.23 and 10.19

3.91 अप्रमेयायुश्चैव सर्वसत्त्वा भवन्तु ते।
नित्यं जीवन्तु सुखिता मृत्युशब्दोऽपि नश्यतु ॥ BCA 10.33

aprameyayuscaiva sarvasattva bhavantu te
nityam jivantu sukhita mrityusabdo'pi nasyatu
—BCA 10.33

Simple meaning—Not only for pregnant women, but for others too – may medical facilities prolong the lifespan of all – of course, a long life is desirable only if people can live happily. BCA 10.33

3.92 सुखभोगबुभुक्षितस्य वा
जनसार्थस्य भवाध्वचारिणः।
सुखसत्रमिदं ह्युपस्थितम्
सकलाभ्यागतसत्त्वतर्पणम् ॥ BCA 3.32

sukhabhogabubhuksitasya va
janasarthasya bhavadhvacarinah
sukhasatramidam hyupasthitam
sakalabhyagatasattvatarpanam —BCA 3.32

Simple meaning—I recognize that all human beings should be able to carry on their lives, experiencing health and happiness. With Buddha's blessing, such a joyful banquet can be prepared for the complete satisfaction of every being who comes to it. BCA 3.32

3.93 नावध्यायन्ति तरवो न चाराध्याः प्रयत्नतः।
कदा तैः सुखसंवासैः सहवासो भवेन्मम ॥ BCA 8.26

navadhyayanti taravo na caradhyah prayatnatah
kada taih sukhasamvasaih sahavaso bhavenmama
—BCA 8.26

Simple meaning—Nature is showing the right way to human beings–for example, trees have their fruit for all, not for themselves. They seek nothing in return. If human beings follow nature, they can learn the lesson of helping all, without discrimination. BCA 8.26

3.94 पाठस्वाध्यायकलिला विहाराः सन्तु सुस्थिताः
नित्यं स्यात् संघसामग्री संघकार्यं च सिध्यतु ।। BCA 10.42
विवेकलाभिनः सन्तु शिक्षाकामाश्च भिक्षवः ।
कर्मण्यचित्ता ध्यायन्तु सर्वविक्षेपवर्जिताः ।। BCA 10.43
लाभिन्यः सन्तु भिक्षुण्यः कलहायासवर्जिताः ।
भवन्त्वखण्डशीलाश्च सर्वे प्रव्रजितास्तथा ।। BCA 10.44

pathasvadhyayakalila viharah santu susthitah
nityam syat sanghasamagri sanghakaryam ca sidhyatu
—BCA 10.42

vivekalabhinah santu siksakamasca bhiksavah
karmanyacitta dhyayantu sarvaviksepavarjitah
—BCA 10.43

labhinyah santu bhiksunyah kalahayasavarjitah
bhavantvakhandasilasca sarve pravrajitastatha
—BCA 10.44

Simple meaning—The monasteries need to ensure equal treatment of monks and nuns – this is a pre-requisite for their success. (For meanings of verses 10.42 and 10.43, please see paras 3.59 and 3.60). May the nuns receive the same honor as the monks, free from discrimination and prejudice. May their practice of self-discipline continue without hindrance. BCA 10.42, 43, 44

Reform rather than punish : Selection from Lotus Sutra

3.95 The most well-known instance relating to 'Reform rather than punish' is provided in chapter 12 entitled "Devadatta". In order to bring out the significance of the narration of chapter 12, we give below background information about Devadatta.

3.96 Devadatta was a cousin of the Buddha. He was converted to the new religion by the Buddha, and the initial years of his monkhood were "normal", as a result of which Devadatta became an esteemed member of the monastic community.

However, he later became a symbol of treachery and evil for the Buddhist tradition. This was a sad phase in Devadatta's life. He attempted to usurp the Buddha's position. At one point he did convince 500 monks to split from the main body of monks and join his (i.e. Devadatta's) group after he introduced five new, austere rules. This created a schism in the Buddhist order. However, the main group loyal to the Buddha countered successfully. Trusted assistants of the Buddha, like Sariputra and Maudgalyayana, were able to convince the schismatic monks to return to the original community.

3.97 At the most treacherous phase of his life, Devadatta conspired with Prince Ajatasatru to replace the reigning King Bimbisara, and to assassinate the Buddha. The king was deposed, but luckily Devadatta's attempt to assassinate the Buddha did not succeed.

3.98 Now the narration of Chapter 12 of Lotus Sutra in which Devadatta is honored (not punished).

अयमेव स तेन कालेन तेन समयेन देवदत्तो भिक्षुः
ऋषिः अभूत्। देवदत्तो हि भिक्षवो मम कल्याणमित्रम्।
देवदत्तमेव चागम्य मया षट पारमिताः परिपूरिताः
महामैत्री महाकरुणा महामुदिता महोपेक्षा
द्वात्रिंशन्महापुरुषलक्षणानि अशीत्यनुव्यंजनानि
सुवर्णवर्णच्छविता दश बलानि चत्वारि वैशारद्यानि
चत्वारि संग्रहवस्तूनि अष्टादशावेणिकबुद्धधर्मा
महाऋद्धिबलता दशदिक्सत्त्वनिस्तारणता
सर्वमेतद् देवदत्तमागस्य। आरोचयामि वो
भिक्षवः प्रतिवेदयामि एष देवदत्तो भिक्षुरनागतेऽध्वनि
अप्रमेयैः कल्पैः असंख्येयैः देवराजो नाम
तथागतोऽर्हन् सम्यक्सम्बुद्धो भविष्यति
विद्याचरणसम्पन्नः सुगतो लोकविदनुत्तरः
पुरुषदम्यसारथिः शास्ता देवानां च मनुष्याणां च
भगवान् देवसोपानायां लोकधातौ ।। LS Chapter 12

ayameva sa tena kalena tena samayena
devadatto bhiksuh risih abhut devadatto hi
bhiksavo mama kalyanamitram devadattameva
cagamya maya sat paramitah paripuritah
mahamaitri mahakaruna mahamudita mahopeksa
dvatrimsanmahapurusalaksanani
asityanuvyanjanani suvarnavarnacchavita
dasa balani catvari vaisaradyani catvari
sangrahavastuni astadasavenikabuddhadharma
mahariddhibalata dasadiksattvanistaranata
sarvametad devadattamagasya arocayami
vo bhiksavah prativedayami esa devadatto
bhiksuranagate' dhvani aprameyaih kalpaih
asamkhyeyaih devarajo nama tathagato' rhan
samyaksambuddho bhavisyati vidyacarana-
-sampannah sugato lokavidanuttarah
purusadamyasarathih sasta devanam ca
manusyanam ca bhagavan devasopanayam
lokadhatau —*LS Chapter 12*

Simple meaning—It was this Devadatta himself, the monk, who at that time, at that juncture, was the Seer. Indeed, Devadatta was my good friend. By the aid of Devadatta have I accomplished the six perfect virtues. noble kindness, noble compassion, noble sympathy, noble impartiality, the thirty-two signs of a great man, the eighty lesser marks, the gold colored tinge, the ten powers, the fourfold absence of hesitation, the four articles of sociability, the eighteen uncommon properties, magical power, ability to save beings in all directions of space—all this have I got after coming to Devadatta. I announce to you, monks, I declare to you: This Devadatta, the monk, will, in an age to come, after a long time, become a Tathagata named Devaraja, in the world Devasopana. LS Chapter 12

Reform rather than punish: Selections from Bodhicaryavatara

3.99 दुःशीलाः सन्तु संविग्नाः पापक्षयरताः सदा।
सुगतेर्लाभिनः सन्तु तत्र चाखण्डितव्रताः ।। BCA 10.45

duhsilah santu samvignah papaksayaratah sada
sugaterlabhinah santu tatra cakhanditavratah

—BCA 10.45

Simple meaning—May the ill-behaved be reformed, and reoriented to get rid of their evil mentality. In this way, may they make a fresh start, ultimately attaining Buddhahood.

BCA 10.45

3.100 भीताश्च निर्भयाः सन्तु शोकार्ताः प्रीतिलाभिनः ।
उद्विग्नाश्च निरुद्वेगा धृतिमन्तो भवन्तु च ।। BCA 10.21

bhitasca nirbhayah santu sokartah pritilabhinah
udvignasca nirudvega dhritimanto bhavantu ca

—BCA 10.21

Simple meaning—May those who are afraid (that they will be punished) get a message of pardon and reform. May those afflicted with sorrow be the obtainers of joy. May those distressed be without distress, and at peace. BCA 10.21

3.101 अंगारतप्तोपलशस्त्रवृष्टिः
अद्यप्रभृत्यस्तु च पुष्पवृष्टिः ।
तच्छस्त्रयुद्धं च परस्परेण
क्रीडार्थमद्यास्तु च पुष्पयुद्धम् ।। BCA 10.9

angarataptopalasastravristih
adyaprabhrityastu ca puspavristih
tacchastrayuddham ca parasparena
kridarthamadyastu ca puspayuddham *—BCA 10.9*

Simple meaning—May the shower of swords, stones, and burning charcoal, be henceforth a flower-rain, and the unceasing battle of swords be afterwards a joyful flower–battle for the sake of sport. BCA 10.9

3.102 कृत्वापि पापानि सुदारुणानि
यदाश्रयादुत्तरति क्षणेन ।

शूराश्रयेणेव महाभयानि
नाश्रीयते तत्कथमज्ञसत्त्वैः ।। BCA 1.13

kritvapi papani sudarunani
yadasrayaduttarati ksanena
surasrayeneva mahabhayani
nasriyate tatkathamajnasattvaih —*BCA 1.13*

Simple meaning—Even those who have committed the most dreadful deeds, can escape from dharmic punishment by going under the protection of the Buddha. In worldly life, the head of state has powers to grant pardon. Dharmic leaders should make this known to all so that lack of such knowledge need not be an obstacle in the way of reform.

BCA 1.13

Chapter 4

Five Methods of Implementing the Message

4.1 In the preceding chapter, we specified and explained the social message of Mahayana Buddhism, by digging deep into the Lotus Sutra and Bodhicaryavatara. The main purpose of writing this book, or rather the first part of the purpose, has thus been accomplished. However, both the scriptures that we have used, recognize the need to give clear instructions to people about the methods of implementing the social message. That aspect constitutes the subject-matter of the present chapter, and is viewed by us as an integral part of the purpose that we have set before us in this book. We will achieve this by making use of a five-way classification of methods, keeping in mind the importance of tackling different types of implementational problems:-

(i) Spreading the message

(ii) Motivation and inspiration

(iii) Non-violent action and perseverance

(iv) Worship and prayer

(v) Meditation and dedication

4.2 As we did in the preceding chapter, here too, for each of the five methods, we have identified relevant portions of the two texts. Again, our presentation will include the Sanskrit text as well as its simple meaning in English.

Spreading the message: Selections from Lotus Sutra

4.3 तत्र भैषज्यराज यः कश्चिदन्यतरः पुरुषो वा
स्त्री वा एवं वदेत् कीदृशाः खल्वपि ते सत्त्वा
भविष्यन्ति अनागतेऽध्वनि तथागता अर्हन्तः
सम्यक्सम्बुद्धा इति। तस्य भैषज्यराज पुरुषस्य
वा स्त्रिया वा स कुलपुत्रो वा कुलदुहिता वा
दर्शयितव्यः य इतो धर्मपर्यायादन्तशश्चतुष्पादिकामपि
गाथां धारयिता श्रावयिता वा देशयिता वा
सगौरवो वेह धर्मपर्याये। अयं स कुलपुत्रो
वा कुलदुहिता वा यो ह्यनागतेऽध्वनि
तथागतोऽर्हन् सम्यक्सम्बुद्धो भविष्यति ।। LS Chapter 10

tatra bhaisajyaraja yah kascidanyatarah puruso va stri va evam vadet kidrisah khalvapi te sattva bhavisyanti anagate' dhvani tathagata arhantah samyaksambuddha iti tasya bhaisajyaraja purusasya va striya va sa kulaputro va kuladuhita va darsayitavyah ya ito dharmaparyayadantasascatuspadikamapi gatham dharayita sravayita va desayita va sagauravo veha dharmaparyaye ayam sa kulaputro va kuladuhita va yo hyanagate' dhvani tathagato'rhan samyaksambuddho bhavisyati

—LS Chapter 10

Simple meaning—Should some man or woman, Bhaisajyaraja, happen to ask: who are the persons that in future will become Tathagatas, Arhats, and Samyaksambuddhas? The most important example of such persons is now specified, viz. that whoever is able to keep, recite, or teach the Lotus Sutra, were it but a single verse of four lines, and whoever shows respect for this Dharmaparyaya–that young man or young woman of good family shall in future become a Tathagata or Arhat or Samyaksambuddha. LS Chapter 10

4.4 तस्येदं दुष्करतरं इदं सूत्रं च धारयेत्।
श्रद्दधेद् अधिमुच्येद् वा भाषेद् वापि पुनः पुनः ।। LS 11.31
चक्षुभूतश्च सो भोति लोके सामरमानुषे।
इदं सूत्रं प्रकाशित्वा निर्वृते नरनायके ।। LS 11.40
वन्दनीयश्च सो भोति लोके सामरमानुषे।
पश्चिमे कालि यो भाषेत् सूत्रमेकं मुहूर्तकम् ।। LS 11.41

tasyedam duskarataram idam sutram ca dharayet
sraddadhed adhimucyed va bhased vapi punah punah —*LS 11.31*
caksubhutasca so bhoti loke samaramanuse
idam sutram prakasitva nirvrite naranayake—*LS 11.40*
vandaniyasca so bhoti loke samaramanuse
pascime kali yo bhaset sutramekam muhurtakam —*LS 11.41*

Simple meaning—It is most important to keep the Lotus Sutra, believe in it, adhere to it, and explain it to people again and again. LS 11.31

He will be the eye of the world, including gods and men, who shall explain the Lotus Sutra to people, after the departure of the Buddha. LS 11.40

He is to be venerated by all beings, the wise man who will preach the Lotus Sutra, even if it were for a single moment. LS 11.41

4.5 स बंधुभूतो भवतीह प्राणिनाम्
आलोकजातो विचरन्तु मेदिनीम्
तिमिरं हरन्तो बहुप्राणकोटिनाम्
यो सूत्रधारे इमु निर्वृते मयि ।। LS 14.59

sa bandhubhuto bhavatiha praninam
alokajato vicarantu medinim
timiram haranto bahu pranakotinam
yo sutradhare imu nirvrite mayi —*LS 14.59*

Simple meaning—The Lord said, "He who keeps the Lotus Sutra after my departure, is a friend to all creatures in the world. He goes all over the earth as a light, dissipating the gloom of millions of creatures." LS 14.59

बहु आनुशंसाश्च अनन्तकाश्च
ये मंजुघोष सदा तस्य भोन्ति।
यो पश्चिमे कालि इममग्रधर्मम्
सूत्रं प्रकाशेय मया सुदेशितम् ।। LS 14.73

bahu anusamsasca anantakasca
ye manjughosa sada tasya bhonti
yo pascime kali imamagradharmam
sutram prakaseya maya sudesitam —LS 14.73

Simple meaning—The Lord said, "Manjughosa, endless are the advantages which constantly are his who at the time of need will expound the Lotus Sutra of superior enlightenment that I have perfectly explained." LS 14.73

4.6 पुण्यस्कंधो अपर्यन्तो वर्णितो मे पुनः पुनः।
य इदं धारयेत् सूत्रं निर्वृते नरनायके ।। LS 17.37
य इदं धारयेत् सूत्रं क्षयकालि च देशयेत्।
ईदृशी मे कृता तेन विविधा पूजनन्तिका ।। LS 17.43
प्रज्ञावांश्चैव धीरश्च प्रश्नं पृष्टो न कुप्यति।
अनुलोमं च देशेति कृपाबुद्धि च प्राणिषु ।। LS 17.55

punyaskandho aparyanto varnito me punah punah
ya idam dharayet sutram nirvrite naranayake —LS 17.37
ya idam dharayet sutram ksayakali ca desayet
idrisi me krita tena vividha pujanantika —LS 17.43
prajnavamscaiva dhirasca prasnam pristo na kupyati
anulomam ca deseti kripabuddhi ca pranisu —LS 17.55

Simple meaning—The Lord said, "An immense mass of merit, as I have repeatedly mentioned, shall be his who, after the departure of the Leader of men, shall keep the Lotus Sutra.

He, who at the period of deprivation, shall keep and teach this Sutra, will have paid me such an infinitely varied worship. Sensible and wise, not angry when he is asked a question, he, full of compassion for all beings, gives such instruction as suits the listeners." LS 17.37, 43, 55

4.7 य इमं सूत्रं भाषेत पर्षासु च विशारदः ।
अनोलीनः प्रकाशेया गुणांस्तस्य शृणुस्व मे ।। LS 19.1
यश्चापि धर्मं शृणुतेऽस्य भाषतो
दृष्टान्तकोटीनयुतैरनेकैः ।
प्रामोद्य तत्रापि जनेति सोऽग्रम्
पूजां च तस्य कुरुतेऽप्रमेयाम् ।। LS 19.54
आचार्यभूमौ हि स्थितश्च भोति
सर्वेश सत्त्वान कथेय धर्मम् ।
निरुक्तिकोटीकुशलश्च भोति
इमु धारयन्तो सुगतस्य सूत्रम् ।। LS 19.76

ya imam sutram bhaseta parsasu ca visaradah
anolinah prakaseya gunamstasya srinusva me—LS 19.1
yascapi dharmam srinute'sya bhasato
dristantakotinayutairanekaih
pramodya tatrapi janeti so'gram
pujam ca tasya kurute' prameyam —LS 19.54
acaryabhumau hi sthitasca bhoti
sarvesa sattvana katheya dharmam
niruktikotikusalasca bhoti
imu dharayanto sugatasya sutram —LS 19.76

Simple meaning—The Lord said, "Hear from me what good qualities will belong to him who, unhesitatingly and undismayed, will preach the Lotus Sutra to the congregated assembly. And whosoever hears him when he is delivering a sermon with lots of examples, feels great joy and shows him immense veneration. He who keeps and teaches this Sutra, stands on the stage of great masters, and he soon becomes skilful in explaining the true Dharma to all categories of common people." LS 19.1, 54, 76

4.8 अथ खलु विशिष्टचारित्रप्रमुखानि बहूनि
बोधिसत्त्वकोटीनयुतशतसहस्राणि भगवन्तमेतदूचुः
वयमपि भगवन् इमं धर्मपर्यायं सम्प्रकाशयिष्यामः
तथागतस्य परिनिर्वृतस्य। अथ खलु भगवान्
तस्यां वेलायां गणाचार्यं आमन्त्रायामास
साधु साधु विशिष्टचारित्र एवं युष्माभिः करणीयं
अस्य धर्मपर्यायस्यार्थे यूयं तथागतेन परिपाचिताः ।। LS Chapter 21

atha khalu visistacaritrapramukhani bahuni bodhisattvakotinayutasatasahasrani bhagavantametaducuh vayamapi bhagavan imam dharmaparyayam samprakasayisyamah tathagatasya parinirvritasya atha khalu bhagavan tasyam velayam ganacaryam amantrayamasa sadhu sadhu visistacaritra evam yusmabhih karaniyam asya dharmaparyayasyarthe yuyam tathagatena paripacitah —*LS Chapter 21*

Simple meaning—A large number of Bodhisattvas, headed by Visistacaritra, said to the Lord, "We also will promulgate the Lotus Sutra after the departure of the Tathagata." Then the Lord addressed the Bodhisattva Mahasattva Visistacaritra, "Very well, very well, I am glad that you will do so; it is for the sake of this Dharmaparyaya that the Tathagata has brought you to ripeness." LS Chapter 21

4.9 द्वैतीयकमपि त्रैतीयकमपि भगवान् सर्वावन्तं बोधिसत्त्वगणं
एतदवोचत् युष्माकं हस्ते परिंदामि अनुपरिंदामि निक्षिपामि
उपनिक्षिपामि युष्माभिः कुलपुत्रा उद्ग्रहीतव्या धारयितव्या
वाचयितव्या पर्यवासव्या देशयितव्या प्रकाशयितव्या
सर्वसत्त्वानां च संश्रावयितव्या अमात्सर्योऽहं कुलपुत्रा
अपरिगृहीतचित्तो विशारदो बुद्धज्ञानस्य दाता
तथागतज्ञानस्य स्वयंभूज्ञानस्य दाता महादानपतिरहं
कुलपुत्रा युष्माभिरपि ममैवानुशिक्षितव्यं
अमत्सरिभिर्भूत्वेमं तथागतज्ञानदर्शनं महोपायकौशल्यं

आगतानां कुलपुत्राणां कुलदुहितॄणां च अयं धर्मपर्याय:
संश्रावयितव्य: ये च अश्राद्धा: सत्वा: तेऽस्मिन्
धर्मपर्याये समादापयितव्या: एवं युष्माभि: कुलपुत्रा
तथागतानां प्रतिकार: कृतो भविष्यति ।। LS Chapter 22

dvaitiyakamapi traitiyakamapi bhagavan sarvavantam bodhisattvaganam etadavocat yusmakam haste parindami anuparindami niksipami upaniksipami yusmabhih kulaputra udgrahitavya dharayitavya vacayitavya paryavaptavya desayitavya prakasayitavya sarvasattvanam ca samsravayitavya amatsaryo'ham kulaputra aparigrihitacitto visarado buddhajnanasya data tathagatajnanasya svayambhujnanasya data mahadanapatiraham kulaputra yusmabhirapi mamaivanusiksitavyam amatsaribhirbhutvemam tathagatajnanadarsanam mahopayakausalyam agatanam kulaputranam kuladuhitrinam ca ayam dharmaparyayah samsravayitavyah ye ca asraddhah sattvah te'smin dharmaparyaye samadapayitavyah evam yusmabhih kulaputra tathagatanam pratikarah krito bhavisyati

—*LS Chapter* 22

Simple meaning—A second time, a third time, the Lord spoke to the host of Bodhisattvas, "Into your hands, young men of good family, I transfer and transmit, entrust and deposit this supreme and perfect Lotus Sutra. Receive it, young men of good family, keep, read, fathom, teach, promulgate, and preach it to all beings. I am not avaricious, young men of good family, nor narrow-minded, I am confident and willing to impart Buddha-knowledge, to impart the knowledge of the Tathagata, the knowledge of the Self-born. I am a bountiful giver, and you should follow my example; imitate me in liberally showing this knowledge of the Tathagata, and in skilfulness, and preach this Dharmaparyaya to the young men and young women of good family who successively will gather round you. And as to unbelieving persons, rouse them to accept this Dharma. By so doing, you will acquit your debt to the Tathagatas. (LS Chapter 22)

4.10 भगवानाह आरोचयामि ते भैषज्यराज प्रतिवेदयामि
यः कश्चिद् कुलपुत्रो वा कुलदुहिता वा अस्मात्
सद्धर्मपुण्डरीकाद् धर्मपर्यायाद् एकामपि
चतुष्पदीगाथां धारयेत् वाचयेत् पर्यवाप्नुयात्
प्रतिपत्त्या च सम्पादयेत् अतः स ततोनिदानं
बहुतरं पुण्यं प्रसवेत् ।। LS Chapter 26

bhagavanaha arocayami te bhaisajyaraja prativedayami
yah kascid kulaputro va kuladuhita va asmat
saddharmapundarikad dharmaparyayad ekamapi
catuspadigatham dharayet vacayet paryavapnuyat
pratipattya ca sampadayet atah sa tatonidanam
bahutaram punyam prasavet

—LS Chapter 26

Simple meaning—The Lord said, "I announce to you, Bhaisajyaraja, I declare to you : any young man or young woman of good family, who will keep, read, comprehend, and in practice follow, even if it were only one verse from the Lotus Sutra–that young man or young woman of good family, will on that account produce far more pious merit (than by merely worshipping the Tathagatas). LS Chapter 26

4.11 भगवान् समन्तभद्रं बोधिसत्त्वं महासत्त्वं महासत्त्वं एतदवोचत्
पण्डितेन कुलपुत्रेण वा कुलदुहिता वा अयं
सद्धर्मपुण्डरीको धर्मपर्यायः सत्कृत्य लिखितव्यः
सत्कृत्योद्देष्टव्यः सत्कृत्य स्वाध्यायितव्यः
सत्कृत्य मनसि कर्तव्यः इमं कुलपुत्रा धर्मपर्यायं
लिखित्वा उद्दिश्य स्वाध्यायित्वा भावयित्वा मनसि कृत्वा एवमप्रमेया गुणा
भविष्यन्ति ।। LS Chapter 28

bhagavan samantabhadram bodhisattvam
mahasattvam etadavocat panditena kulaputrena

va kuladuhita va ayam saddharmapundariko dharmaparyayah satkritya likhitavyah satkrityoddestavyah satkritya svadhyayitavyah satkritya manasi kartavyah imam kulaputra dharmaparyayam likhitva uddisya svadhyayitva bhavayitva manasi kritva evamaprameya guna bhavisyanti —*LS Chapter 28*

Simple meaning—The Lord said to the Bodhisattva Mahasattva Samantabhadra, "A wise young man or young woman of good family should respectfully write this Dharmaparyaya of the Lotus Sutra, respectfully recite it, respectfully study it, respectfully treasure it up in his (or her) mind. By writing, reciting, and studying it, and by treasuring it up in one's mind, one acquires innumerable good qualities." LS Chapter 28

Spreading the message : Selections from Bodhicaryavatara

4.12 यथा गृहीतं सुगतैः बोधिचित्तं पुरातनैः ।
ते बोधिसत्त्वशिक्षायामानुपूर्व्या यथा स्थिताः ।। BCA 3.22
तद् वदुत्पादयाम्येष बोधिचित्तं जगद् हिते
तद्वदेव च ताः शिक्षाः शिक्षिष्यामि यथाक्रमम् ।। BCA 3.23

yatha grihitam sugataih bodhicittam puratanaih
te bodhisattvasiksayamanupurvya yatha sthitah —BCA 3.22
tad vadutpadayamyesa bodhicittam jagad hite
tadvadeva ca tah siksah siksisyami yathakramam
—BCA 3.23

Simple meaning—Following the example of the Bodhisattvas, who recognized the importance of education, I am directing bodhicitta to the cause of "good of the world" and I will promote this idea by teaching and spreading this message. BCA 3.22-23

Motivation and inspiration : Selections from Lotus Sutra

4.13 समन्तभद्र अस्य धर्मपर्यायस्य धारकाणां भिक्षूणां
दूरत एव प्रत्युत्थातव्यम् । यथा तथागतस्यान्तिके

गौरवं कर्तव्यं तथा तेषामेव सूत्रान्तधारकाणां
भिक्षूणां एवं गौरवं कर्तव्यम् ।। LS Chapter 28

samantabhadra asya dharmaparyayasya dharakanam bhiksunam durata eva pratyutthatavyam. yatha tathagatasyantike gauravam kartavyam tatha tesameva sutrantadharakanam bhiksunam evam gauravam kartavyam —*LS Chapter 28*

Simple meaning—The Lord said, "Samantabhadra, people should, even from afar, rise from their seats, as a mark of respect for the monks who teach the Lotus Sutra. Showing them the same reverence as to the Tathagata, will motivate and inspire the preachers of the Lotus Sutra." LS Chapter 28

Motivation and inspiration: Selections from Bodhicaryavatara

4.14 Chapter one of Bodhicaryavatara is entited "Bodhicitta-anusamsa" which can be translated as "In praise of the thought of enlightnment". A large part of the chapter provides material that is appropriate to what we have called "Motivation and inspiration". In order not to interfere with the continuity that underlies Shantideva's presentation, we shall keep the same order of verses that exists in Bodhicaryavatara.

4.15 सुगतान् ससुतान् सधर्मकायान्
प्रणिपत्यादरतोऽखिलांश्च वंद्यान् ।
सुगतात्मजसंवरावतारम्
कथयिष्यामि यथागमं समासात् ।। BCA 1.1

sugatan sasutan sadharmakayan
pranipatyadarato' khilamsca vandyan
sugatatmajasamvaravataram
kathayisyami yathagamam samasat —*BCA 1.1*

Simple meaning—Bowing respectfully to the Buddhas, the Bodhisattvas, and to all others (because ultimately they too will attain enlightenment), I will relate briefly, how our scriptures narrate the spiritual journey of an aspirant (that starts with motivation). BCA 1.1

4.16 न हि किंचिद् अपूर्वमत्र वाच्यम्
न च संग्रथनकौशलं ममास्ति।
अत एव न मे परार्थचिन्ता
स्वमनो वासयितुं कृतं मयेदम्।। BCA 1.2

na hi kincid apurvamatra vacyam
na ca sangrathanakausalam mamasti
ata eva na me pararthacinta
svamano vasayitum kritam mayedam —*BCA 1.2*

Simple meaning—There is nothing original here, and I have no skill in literary composition. I have composed this with no thought of any other purpose than to give peace to my own mind. BCA 1.2

4.17 मम तावदनेन याति वृद्धिम्
कुशलं भावयितुं प्रसादवेगः।
अथ मत्समधातुरेव पश्येद्
अपरोऽप्येनमतोऽपि सार्थकोऽयम् ।। BCA 1.3

mama tavadanena yati vriddhim
kusalam bhavayitum prasadavegah
atha matsamadhatureva pasyed
aparo'pyenamato'pi sarthako'yam —*BCA 1.3*

Simple meaning—The pure impetus to become good is strengthened in me because of this effort to write. Furthermore, if another person like me would like to start the enlightenment–bound journey, he too might get motivated (by reading what I am writing now). BCA 1.3

4.18 क्षणसंपदियं सुदुर्लभा
प्रतिलब्धा पुरुषार्थसाधनी।
यदि नात्र विचिन्त्यते हितम्
पुनरप्येषः समागमः कुतः ।। BCA 1.4

ksanasampadiyam sudurlabha
pratilabdha purusarthasadhani
yadi natra vicintyate hitam
punarapyesah samagamah kutah —*BCA 1.4*

Simple meaning—This favorable moment, so hard to obtain, has arrived, leading to the achievement of man's well-being. If it is not utilized advantageously now, will the opportunity ever come again? BCA 1.4

4.19 रात्रौ यथा मेघघनान्धकारे
विद्युत् क्षणं दर्शयति प्रकाशम्।
बुद्धानुभावेन तथा कदाचिद्
लोकस्य पुण्येषु गतिः क्षणं स्यात् ।। BCA 1.5

ratrau yatha meghaghanandhakare
vidyut ksanam darsayati prakasam
buddhanubhavena tatha kadacid
lokasya punyesu gatih ksanam syat —*BCA 1.5*

Simple meaning—As lightning is seen brightly for an instant in the darkness of a clouded night, so perhaps, for once, the thought of the world may be turned, by the grace of the Buddha, to do good things. BCA 1.5

4.20 तस्मात् शुभं दुर्बलमेव नित्यम्
बलं तु पापस्य महत्सुघोरम्।
तज्जीयतेऽन्येन शुभेन केन
सम्बोधिचित्तं यदि नाम न स्यात् ।। BCA 1.6

tasmat subham durbalameva nityam
balam tu papasya mahatsughoram
tajjiyate' nyena subhena kena
sambodhicittam yadi nama na syat —*BCA 1.6*

Simple meaning—In worldly life, evil forces appear to be overpowering the forces of good. Human capacity to turn the tide in favor of the good can be generated by welcoming the arrival of the thought of enlightenment. BCA 1.6

4.21 कल्पाननल्पान् प्रविचिन्तयद्भिः
दृष्टं मुनीन्द्रैः हितमेतदेव।
यतः सुखेनैव सुखं प्रवृद्धम्
उत्प्लावयत्यप्रमितांजनौघान् ।। BCA 1.7

kalpananalpan pravicintayadbhih
dristam munindraih hitametadeva
yatah sukhenaiva sukham pravriddham
utplavayatyapramitanjanaughan —*BCA 1.7*

Simple meaning—This possibility of turning the tide in favor of the good was discovered by the great sages after reflecting on the problem for many kalpas. Thus the possibility of heaping happiness upon happiness is there, and happiness can be the experience of all humanity. BCA 1.7

4.22 भवदु:खशतानि तर्तुकामै:
अपि सत्त्वव्यसनानि हर्तुकामै: ।
बहुसौख्यशतानि भोक्तुकामै:
न विमोच्यं हि सदैव बोधिचित्तम् ।। BCA 1.8

bhavaduhkhasatani tartukamaih
api sattvavyasanani hartukamaih
bahusaukhyasatani bhoktukamaih
na vimocyam hi sadaiva bodhicittam —*BCA 1.8*

Simple meaning—Never is the thought of Enlightenment to be relinquished by those who are desirous of escaping the hundreds of sources of existence, by those who are desirous of taking upon themselves the suffering of beings, or by those who are desirous of enjoying hundreds of pleasures.
BCA 1.8

4.23 भवचारकबंधनो वराक:
सुगतानां सुत उच्यते क्षणेन ।
सनरामरलोकवंदनीयो
भवति स्मोदिता एव बोधिचित्ते ।। BCA 1.9

bhavacarakabandhano varakah
sugatanam suta ucyate ksanena
sanaramaralokavandaninyo
bhavati smodita eva bodhicitte —*BCA 1.9*

Simple meaning—When the thought of Enlightenment has arisen in a person's mind, people's attitude towards him changes drastically, for example, the wretched one who is bound by the fetters of existence, is instantly proclaimed a son of the Buddhas, and he becomes worthy of being praised in the worlds of men and of immortals. BCA 1.9

4.24 अशुचिप्रतिमां इमां गृहीत्वा
जिनरत्नप्रतिमां करोत्यनर्घाम्।
रसजात्मतीव वेधनीयम्
सुदृढं घृणत बोधिचित्तसंज्ञाम् ।। BCA 1.10

asucipratimam imam grihitva
jinaratnapratimam karotyanargham
rasajatmativa vedhaniyam
sudridham ghrinata bodhicittasanjnam —*BCA 1.10*

Simple meaning—It is important to change one's own attitude towards oneself, for example, give up the feeling that you are impure, and instead of that, feel that you are the Buddha's jewel. This can be done by seizing firmly that very lively elixir which comes to you in the form of the thought of Enlightenment. BCA 1.10

4.25 सुपरीक्षितं अप्रमेयधीभि:
बहुमूल्यं जगदेकसार्थवाहै:।
गतिपत्तनविप्रवासशील:
सुदृढं घृणत बोधिचित्तरत्नम्।। BCA 1.11

supariksitam aprameyadhibhih
bahumulyam jagadekasarthavahaih
gatipattanavipravasasilah
sudridham ghrinata bodhicittaratnam —*BCA 1.11*

Simple meaning—It is important to change your own vision, for example, don't think that you are wandering around in the market places of destiny; in stead of that, view yourself as seizing firmly the priceless jewel which has come to you in the form of the thought of Enlightenment. This jewel has been certified as genuine by the leaders of humanity. BCA 1.11

4.26 कदलीव फलं विहाय याति
क्षयमन्यत् कुशलं हि सर्वमेव।
सततं फलति क्षयं न याति
प्रसवत्येव तु बोधिचित्तवृक्षः ।। BCA 1.12

kadaliva phalam vihaya yati
ksayamanyat kusalam hi sarvameva
satatam phalati ksayam na yati
prasavatyeva tu bodhicittavriksah —BCA 1.12

Simple meaning—The thought of Enlightenment is like a heavenly tree which is permanent and which bears fruit perpetually. Don't compare it with a worldly tree like banana, which gives fruit only once and which decays. BCA 1.12

4.27 तद्बोधिचित्तं द्विविधं विज्ञातव्यं समासतः।
बोधिप्रणिधिचित्तं च बोधिप्रस्थानमेव च ।। BCA 1.15

tadbodhicittam dvividham vijnatavyam samasatah
bodhipranidhicittam ca bodhiprasthanameva ca
—BCA 1.15

Simple meaning—There are two aspects of this thought of Enlightenment. The first one is the thought of the vow of Enlightenment. The second aspect is the actual march towards Enlightenment. BCA 1.15

4.28 गन्तुकामस्य गन्तुश्च यथा भेदः प्रतीयते।
तथा भेदोऽनयोर्ज्ञेयो याथासंख्येन पण्डितैः ।। BCA 1.16

gantukamasya gantusca yatha bhedah pratiyate
tatha bhedo'nayorjneyo yathasamkhyena panditaih
—BCA 1.16

Simple meaning—The difference between the two aspects of the thought of Enlightenment, has been explained by learned men by means of an example, namely, someone desirous of traveling (the first aspect), and some one actually on the move (the second aspect). BCA 1.16

4.29 बोधिप्रणिधिचित्तस्य संसारेऽपि फलं महत्।
न तु अविच्छिन्नपुण्यत्वं यथा प्रस्थानचेतसः ।। BCA 1.17
bodhipranidhicittasya samsare'pi phalam mahat
na tu avicchinnapunyatvam yatha prasthanacetasah
—BCA 1.17

Simple meaning—Undoubtedly, the benefit obtained by the person who is on the move, is superb, yet the benefit obtained by the person who has the desire to travel, should not be under-estimated. BCA 1.17

4.30 यतः प्रभृति अपर्यन्तसत्त्वधातुप्रमोक्षणे।
समाददाति तच्चित्तं अनिवर्त्येन चेतसा ।। BCA 1.18
ततः प्रभृति सुप्तस्य प्रमत्तस्याप्यनेकशः।
अविच्छन्नाः पुण्यधाराः प्रवर्तन्ते नभःसमाः ।। BCA 1.19
yatah prabhriti aparyantasattvadhatupramoksane
samadadati taccittam anivartyena cetasa —BCA 1.18
tatah prabhriti suptasya pramattasyapyanekasah
avicchannah punyadharah pravartante nabhahsamah
—BCA 1.19

Simple meaning—The determination, that I will free myself from the normal bonds of samsara, is the important step—as soon as that step is taken, the door to unlimited merit is opened (and obstacles due to laziness and inertia will not be real obstacles). BCA 1.18-19

4.31 शिरः शूलानि सत्त्वानां नाशयामीति चिन्तयन्।
अप्रमेयेण पुण्येन गृह्यते स्म हिताशयः ।। BCA 1.21
किमुताप्रतिमं शूलं एकैकस्य जिहीर्षतः।
अप्रमेयगुणं सत्त्वं एकैकं च चिकीर्षतः ।। BCA 1.22
sirah sulani sattvanam nasayamiti cintayan
aprameyena punyena grihyate sma hitasayah —BCA 1.21
kimutapratimam sulam ekaikasya jihirsatah
aprameyagunam sattvam ekaikam ca cikirsatah —BCA 1.22

Simple meaning—Even the thought of doing a limited amount of good work (like the desire to remove the grief of some people), brings in great merit, although the ultimate aim has to be to attain the bodhisattva-nature (viz., the vow to remove the grief of every being.) BCA 1.21-22

4.32 कृते यः प्रतिकुर्वीत सोऽपि तावत् प्रशस्यते।
अव्यापारितसाधुस्तु बोधिसत्त्वः किमुच्यताम् ।। BCA 1.31

krite yah pratikurvita so'pi tavat prasasyate
avyaparitasadhustu bodhisattvah kimucyatam —*BCA 1.31*

Simple meaning—The world rightly admires a person who reciprocates for a service rendered. But there are no words to describe the greatness of a bodhisattva whose approach is non-commercial, that is, he does good to all, unconditionally. BCA 1.31

4.33 कतिपयजनसत्रदायकः
कुशलकृदिति अभिपूज्यते जनैः।
क्षणमशनकमात्रदानतः
सपरिभवं दिवसार्धयापनात् ।। BCA 1.32
किमु निरवधिसत्त्वसंख्यया
निरवधिकालमनुप्रयच्छतः।
गगनजनपरिक्षयाक्षयम्
सकलमनोरथसम्प्रपूरणम् ।। BCA 1.33

katipayajanasatradayakah
kusalakriditi abhipujyate janaih
ksanamasanakamatradanatah
saparibhavam divasardhayapanat —*BCA 1.32*
kimu niravadhisattvasamkhyaya
niravadhikalamanuprayacchatah
gaganajana pariksayaksayam
sakalamanorathasamprapuranam —*BCA 1.33*

Simple meaning—The greatness of the bodhisattva-vow is stressed here, by contrasting it with those who do good on a smaller scale.

The one who gives a feast for a few men is honored by those who say that he is a doer of good, although he only supports life for half a day by giving a limited amount of food, to a few people. BCA 1.32

This is nothing in comparison to the bodhisattva who gives, for unlimited time, to unlimited number of beings, that full satisfaction of total desire, which is imperishable, even when the inhabitants of heaven perish. BCA 1.33

4.34 In addition to the verses of Chapter One (of Bodhicaryavatara), there are verses of other chapters too that "motivate and inspire". These are presented below.

4.35 परचोदनदक्षाणां अनधीष्टोपकारिणाम्।
प्रतीच्छेत् शिरसा वाक्यं सर्वशिष्यः सदा भवेत् ।। BCA 5.74
सुभाषितेषु सर्वेषु साधुकारमुदीरयेत्।
पुण्यकारिणं आलोक्य स्तुतिभिः सम्प्रहर्षयेत्।। BCA 5.75

paracodanadaksanam anadhistopakarinam
praticchet sirasa vakyam sarvasisyah sada bhavet
—BCA 5.74

subhasitesu sarvesu sadhukaramudirayet
punyakarinam alokya stutibhih sampraharsayet
—BCA 5.75

Simple meaning—Motivation to do good, can come from those who help others without being asked. For this it is necessary, of course, that one accepts the teaching of such great persons, and is mentally prepared to be their pupil. BCA 5.74

One should admire and say "Excellent", for all that is well spoken. Having seen those achieving merit by good deeds, one should joyfully get the desire to follow in their footsteps. BCA 5.75

4.36 बोधिचित्तं समुत्पाद्य सर्वसत्त्वसुखेच्छया।
त्रैलोक्यपूज्यं बुद्धत्वं सत्त्वानां किल वांछसि।। BCA 6.80-81

bodhicittam samutpadya sarvasattvasukhecchaya
trailokyapujyam buddhatvam sattvanam kila
vamchasi —*BCA 6.80-81*

Simple meaning—Once you are motivated to cultivate the thought of enlightenment, you always desire that all the beings–without any exception–should be happy. Such universality arises automatically when Buddhahood is your goal. BCA 6.80-81

4.37 आशयस्य च माहात्म्यं न स्वत: किं तु कार्यत: ।
समं च तेन माहात्म्यं सत्त्वानां तेन ते समा: ।। BCA 6.114 ।।
asayasya ca mahatmyam na svatah kim tu karyatah
samam ca tena mahatmyam sattvanam tena te samah
—*BCA 6.114*

Simple meaning—The greatness of a person's goodness becomes particularly valuable if it motivates others. It is not important from where the motivation comes; whichever source strikes the chord in our mind, is to be considered great. BCA 6.114

4.38 यदि दास्यामि किं भोक्ष्ये इत्यात्मार्थे पिशाचता ।
यदि भोक्ष्ये किं ददामीति परार्थे देवराजता ।। BCA 8.125
yadi dasyami kim bhoksye ityatmarthe pisacata
yadi bhoksye kim dadamiti pararthe devarajata
—*BCA 8.125*

Simple meaning—Motivation and a change in the thought process go together. Prior to motivation, one thinks, "What shall I have for my own enjoyment, if I spend my resources in helping others?" After motivation, one thinks, "What shall I be able to give to others, if I exhaust my resources in my own enjoyment?" Symbolically, you change your thought process, from that of a demon to that of a god. BCA 8.125

आत्मार्थं पीडयित्वा अन्यं नरकादिषु पच्यते ।
आत्मानं पीडयित्वा तु परार्थं सर्वसम्पद: ।। BCA 8.126

atmartham pidayitva anyam narakadisu pacyate
atmanam pidayitva tu parartham sarvasampadah

—BCA 8.126

Simple meaning—Such a change in the process of thought or action can be visualized in another way too. For example, before motivation, one might be willing to harm others, for one's own benefit. After motivation, one would be willing to harm oneself, for the benefit of others. BCA 8.126

4.39 The above verse of Shantideva is obviously a summary of the following verse of Bhartrihari :

एते सत्पुरुषाः परार्थघटकाः
स्वार्थान् परित्यज्य ये।
सामान्यास्तु परार्थमुद्यमभृतः
स्वार्थाविरोधेन ये।
तेऽमी मानुषराक्षसाः परहितं
स्वार्थाय निघ्नन्ति ये।
ये निघ्नन्ति निरर्थकं परहितं
ते के न जानीमहे।।

ete satpurusah pararthaghatakah
svarthan parityajya ye
samanyastu pararthamudyamabhritah
svarthavirodhena ye
te'mi manusaraksasah parahitam
svarthaya nighnanti ye
ye nighnanti nirarthakam parahitam
te ke na janimahe

Simple meaning—Those who take care of the good of others, even at the cost of their own, I call them 'good'. Those who are engaged in tasks that benefit others, but do not put their own interests at risk, I call them 'ordinary'. Those who work contrary to the good of others, in order to promote their own, I call them 'demons' that look like human beings. Those who destroy what might do good to others, and do this without any valid reason (i.e. even though their own interests might be hurt at the same time), I do not know what to call them (because they are worse than demons.)

4.40 न नाम साध्यं बुद्धत्वं संसारेऽपि कुतः सुखं।
स्वसुखस्य अन्यदुःखेन परिवर्तमकुर्वतः ।। BCA 8.131

na nama sadhyam buddhatvam samsare'pi kutah sukham
svasukhasya anyaduhkhena parivartamakurvatah

—*BCA 8.131*

Simple meaning—Motivation for the thought of Buddha-hood goes hand-in-hand with the willingness to exchange one's own happiness for the sorrow of other people. BCA 8.131

4.41 अभविष्यदिदं कर्म कृतं पूर्वं यदि त्वया।
बौद्धं संपत्सुखं मुक्त्वा नाभविष्यदियं दशा ।। BCA 8.157

abhavisyadidam karma kritam purvam yadi tvaya
bauddham sampatsukham muktva nabhavisyadiyam dasa

—*BCA 8.157*

Simple meaning—Motivation to change the thought process goes hand-in-hand with the realization that, if you previously had made this to be your object—a striving for the attainment of Buddha–hood—liberation would have occurred, and this pitiable condition of life would not have occurred. BCA 8.157

4.42 नावध्यायन्ति तरवो न चाराध्याः प्रयत्नतः।
कदा तैः सुखसंवासैः सह वासो भवेन्मम।। BCA 8.26

navadhyayanti taravo na caradhyah prayatnatah
kada taih sukhasamvasaih saha vaso bhavenmama

—*BCA 8.26*

Simple meaning—Motivation to become helpful for others, can come from nature too. For example, trees have their fruits for others, not for themselves. They seek nothing in return. BCA 8.26

This verse is obviously a summary of the well-known Sanskrit verse:-

स्वयं न खादन्ति फलानि वृक्षाः
पिबन्ति नाम्भः स्वयमेव नद्यः।
धाराधरो वर्षति नात्महेतोः
परोपकाराय सतां विभूतिः ।।

svayam na khadanti phalani vriksah
pibanti nambhah svayameva nadyah
dharadharo varsati natmahetoh
paropakaraya satam vibhutih.

Simple meaning—Trees do not eat their fruits, themselves. Rivers do not drink their water, themselves. Clouds do not pour down their water, for themselves. The capability of good people is used for the good of others.

Non-violent action and perseverance: Selections from Lotus Sutra.

4.43 उपायकौशल्य ममैवरूपम्
यत् त्रीणि यानान्युपदर्शयामि।
एकं तु यानं हि नयश्च एकः
एका चियं देशन नायकानाम् ।। LS 2.69

upayakausalya mamaivarupam
yat trini yananyupadarsayami
ekam tu yanam hi nayasca ekah
eka ciyam desana nayakanam *—LS 2.69*

Simple meaning—The Lord said, "It is my skilfulness which prompts me to manifest three vehicles; for there is but one vehicle and one method; there is also but one instruction by the leaders." LS 2.69

4.44 सर्वेहि तेहि पुरुषोत्तमेहि
प्रकाशिता धर्म बहू विशुद्धाः।
दृष्टान्तकैः कारणहेतुभिश्च
उपायकौशल्यशतैरनेकैः ।। LS 2.72

sarvehi tehi purusottamehi
prakasita dharma bahu visuddhah

dristantakaih karanahetubhisca
upayakausalyasatairanekaih —*LS 2.72*

Simple meaning—Those highest of men (Purusottama) have all of them revealed the holy Dharma by means of illustrations, reasons, and arguments, with many hundred proofs of skilfulness. LS 2.72

सर्वे च ते दर्शयि एकयानम्
एकं च यानं अवतारयन्ति।
एकस्मि याने परिपाचयन्ति
अचिन्त्य प्राणिसहस्रकोट्यः ।। LS 2.73

sarve ca te darsayi ekayanam
ekam ca yanam avatarayanti
ekasmi yane paripacayanti
acintya pranisahasrakotyah —*LS 2.73*

Simple meaning—And all of them have manifested but one vehicle and introduced but one vehicle on earth; by one vehicle have they led to full ripeness, inconceivably large numbers of beings. LS 2.73

अन्ये उपाया विविधा जिनानाम्
येही प्रकाशेन्तिममग्रधामम्।
ज्ञात्वाधिमुक्तिं तथा आशयं च
तथागता लोकि सदेवकस्मिन् ।। LS 2.74

anye upaya vividha jinanam
yehi prakasentimamagradhamam
jnatvadhimuktim tatha asayam ca
tathagata loki sadevakasmin —*LS 2.74*

Simple meaning—Yet the Buddhas and Bodhisattvas possess various and manifold means through which the Tathagata reveals to the world, including the gods, superior enlightenment, in consideration of the inclinations and dispositions of the different beings. LS 2.74

4.45 अनागतापि बहुबुद्धकोट्यो
अचिन्तिया येषु प्रमाणु नास्ति।

तेऽपि जिना उत्तमलोकनाथा:
प्रकाशयिष्यन्ति उपायमेतम् ।। LS 2.98

anagatapi bahubuddhakotyo
acintiya yesu pramanu nasti
te'pi jina uttamalokanathah
prakasayisyanti upayametam —*LS 2.98*

Simple meaning—In future also, the Buddhas and the Bodhisattvas (whose numbers can not even be imagined) will make use of skilful devices, which they will consider appropriate at those times. LS 2.98

उपायकौशल्यमनन्तु तेषाम्
भविष्यति लोकविनायकानाम् ।
येना विनेश्यन्तीह प्राणकोट्यो
बौद्धस्मि ज्ञानस्मि अनास्रवस्मिन् ।। LS 2.99

upayakausalyamanantu tesam
bhavisyati lokavinayakanam
yena vinesyantiha pranakotyo
bauddhasmi jnanasmi anasravasmin —*LS 2.99*

Simple meaning—Endless will be the skilfulness of these leaders of the world, by which they will educate countless beings to the true Buddha-knowledge which is free from imperfection. LS 2.99

एकोऽपि सत्त्वो न कदाचि तेषाम्
श्रुत्वान धर्मं न भवेत बुद्धः ।
प्रणिधानमेतद्धि तथागतानाम्
चरित्व बोधाय चरापयेयम् ।। LS 2.100

eko'pi sattvo na kadaci tesam
srutvana dharmam na bhaveta buddhah
pranidhanametaddhi tathagatanam
caritva bodhaya carapayeyam —*LS 2.100*

Simple meaning—Never has there been any being who, after being educated in the true Dharma, has not attained Enlightenment; for this is the supreme vow of the Tathagatas:

"I will, by accomplishing my plan of work and skilfulness, lead every one to Enlightenment." LS 2.100

4.46 स्थितिका हि एषा सदा धर्मनेत्री
प्रकृतिश्च कौशल्य सदा प्रभासते।
विदित्व बुद्धा द्विपदानमुत्तमा
प्रकाशयिष्यन्ति ममैकयानम् ।। LS 2.102

sthitika hi esa sada dharmanetri
prakritisca kausalya sada prabhasate
viditva buddha dvipadanamuttama
prakasayisyanti mamaikayanam —*LS 2.102*

Simple meaning—The tradition of the Dharma displays an unbroken continuity, but the nature of skilfulness is adapted to circumstances. Knowing this, the Buddhas, the highest of men, will reveal this single vehicle. LS 2.102

धर्मस्थितिं धर्मनियामतां च
नित्यस्थितां लोकि इमामकम्प्याम्।
बुद्धाश्च बोधिं पृथिवीय मण्डे
प्रकाशयिष्यन्ति उपायकौशलम् ।। LS 2.103

dharmasthitim dharmaniyamatam ca
nityasthitam loki imamakampyam
buddhasca bodhim prithiviya mande
prakasayisyanti upayakausalam —*LS 2.103*

Simple meaning—The Buddhas will reveal the stability of the Dharma, its adherence to fixed rules, its unshakeable perpetuity in the world, the presence of the bodhisattvas on the elevated terrace of the earth, and their skilfulness.
LS 2.103

दशसु दिशासु नरदेवपूजिताः
तिष्ठन्ति बुद्धा यथा गंगवालिकाः।
सुखापनार्थं इह सर्वप्राणिनाम्
ते चापि भाषन्तिममग्रबोधिम् ।। LS 2.104

dasasu disasu naradevapujitah
tisthanti buddha yatha gangavalikah
sukhapanartham iha sarvapraninam
te capi bhasantimamagrabodhim —*LS 2.104*

Simple meaning—The Buddhas exist in all directions of space, like sand of the Ganges River, honored by gods and men; everywhere the Buddhas expound superior Enlightenment, for the happiness of all beings in the world. LS 2.104

उपायकौशल्य प्रकाशयन्ति
विविधानि यानान्युपदर्शयन्ति।
एकं च यानं परिदीपयन्ति
बुद्धा इमामुत्तमशान्तभूमिम् ।। LS 2.105

upayakausalya prakasayanti
vividhani yananyupadarsayanti
ekam ca yanam paridipayanti
buddha imamuttamasantabhumim —*LS 2.105*

Simple meaning—Those Buddhas make use of skilfulness while displaying various vehicles, but all the time, they confirm the one single vehicle, the supreme vehicle leading to Enlightenment and Bliss. LS 2.105

4.47 ततो ह्यहं शारिसुता विदित्वा
वाराणसीं प्रस्थितु तस्मि काले।
तहि पंचकानां प्रवदामि भिक्षुणाम्
धर्मं उपायेन प्रशान्तभूमिम् ।। LS 2.125

tato hyaham sarisuta viditva
varanasim prasthitu tasmi kale
tahi pancakanam pravadami bhiksunam
dharmam upayena prasantabhumim —*LS 2.125*

Simple meaning—The Lord said, "O Sariputra, I made use of skilfulness at Varanasi (Benares) when I preached the Dharma to the five disciples, keeping in mind people's desire for peace." LS 2.125

ततः प्रवृत्तं मम धर्मचक्रम्
निर्वाणशब्दश्च अभूषि लोके।
अर्हन्तशब्दस्तथा धर्मशब्दः
संघस्य शब्दश्च अभूषि तत्र ।। LS 2.126

tatah pravrittam mama dharmacakram
nirvanasabdasca abhusi loke
arhantasabdastatha dharmasabdah
sanghasya sabdasca abhusi tatra —*LS 2.126*

Simple meaning—From that moment, the wheel of my Dharma has been moving, and the name of Nirvana made its appearance in the world, as well as the name of Arhat, of Dharma, and of Sangha. LS 2.126

उपसंक्रमित्वा च ममैव अन्तिके
कृतांजलिः सर्वि स्थिताः सगौरवाः।
येही श्रुतो धर्म जिनान आसीत्
उपायकौशल्यु बहुप्रकारम् ।। LS 2.129

upasamkramitva ca mamaiva antike
kritanjalih sarvi sthitah sagauravah
yehi sruto dharma jinana asit
upayakausalyu bahuprakaram —*LS 2.129*

Simple meaning—Those who had heard the Dharma based on Nirvana, owing to the many-sidedness of their skilfulness, approached me and stood before my face, all of them with prayer-ful posture, and respectful (pleading for the revelation of bodhisattva-based Dharma.) LS 2.129

ततो ममा एतदभूषि तत्क्षणम्
समयो ममा भाषितुमग्रधर्मम्।
यस्याहमर्थं इह लोकि जातः
प्रकाशयामि तमिहाग्रबोधिम् ।। LS 2.130

tato mama etadabhusi tatksanam
samayo mama bhasitumagradharmam

yasyahamartham iha loki jatah
prakasayami tamihagrabodhim —*LS 2.130*

Simple meaning—Then I became convinced that the right time has arrived for me, to use skilfulness and to announce the bodhisattva-based dharma, for which task I was born in the world. LS 2.130

4.48 अथ खलु भैषज्यराजो बोधिसत्त्वो महासत्त्वो
महाप्रतिभानश्च बोधिसत्त्वो महासत्त्वो
विंशतिबोधिसत्त्वशतसहस्रपरिवारो भगवतः
सम्मुखमिमां वाचमभाषेता अल्पोत्सुको भगवान्
भवतु अस्मिन्नर्थे वयमिमं भगवन् धर्मपर्यायं
तथागतस्य परिनिर्वृतस्य सत्त्वानां देशयिष्यामः
सम्प्रकाशयिष्यामः किंचापि भगवन् शठकाः सत्त्वाः
तस्मिन् काले भविष्यन्ति परीत्तकुशलमूला अधिमानिका
लाभसत्कारसंनिश्रिता अकुशलमूलप्रतिपन्ना दुर्दमा
अधिमुक्तिविरहिता अनधिमुक्तिबहुलाः अपि तु खलु
पुनर्वयं भगवन् क्षान्तिबलं उपदर्शयित्वा तस्मिन्
काले इदं सूत्रं उद्देक्ष्यामो धारयिष्यामो देशयिष्यामो
लिखिष्यामः सत्करिष्यामो गुरुकरिष्यामो
मानयिष्यामः पूजयिष्यामः कायजीवितं च वयं
भगवन् उत्सृज्य इदं सूत्रं प्रकाशयिष्यामः अल्पोत्सुको
भगवान् भवतु इति। अथ खलु तस्यां पर्षदि
शैक्षाशैक्षाणां भिक्षूणां पंचमात्राणि भिक्षुशतानि
भगवन्तं एतदूचुः वयमपि भगवन् उत्सहामहे इमं
धर्मपर्यायं सम्प्रकाशयितुं अपि तु खलु पुनर्भगवन्
अन्यासु लोकधातुषु इति ।। LS Chapter 13

atha khalu bhaisajyarajo bodhisattvo mahasattvo
mahapratibhanasca bodhisattvo mahasattvo
vimsatibodhisattvasatasahasraparivaro bhagavatah
sammukhamimam vacamabhaseta alpotsuko
bhagavan bhavatu asminnarthe vayamimam
bhagavan dharmaparyayam tathagatasya

parinirvritasya sattvanam desayisyamah
samprakasayisyamah kimcapi bhagavan
sathakah sattvah tasmin kale bhavisyanti
parittakusalamula adhimanika labhasatkaresamnisrita
akusalamulapratipanna durdama
adhimuktivirahita anadhimuktibahulah api tu
khalu punarvayam bhagavan ksantibalam
upadarsayitva tasmin kale idam sutram uddeksyamo
dharayisyamo desayisyamo likhisyamah
satkarisyamo gurukrisyamo manayisyamah
pujayisyamah kayajivitam ca vayam bhagavan
utsrijya idam sutram prakasayisyamah
alpotsuko bhagavan bhavatu iti atha khalu
tasyam parsadi saiksasaiksanam bhiksunam
pancamatrani bhiksusatani bhagavantam etaducuh
vayamapi bhagavan utsamahe imam dharmaparyayam
samprakasayitum api tu khalu punarbhagavan
anyasu lokadhatusu iti —*LS Chapter 13*

Simple meaning—Bodhisattva Bhaisajyaraja and Bodhisattva Mahapratibhana, with a retinue of twenty hundred thousand Bodhisattvas, spoke before the face of the Lord the following words: Let the Lord be at ease in this respect; we will, after the departure of the Tathagata, expound this Dharma to all beings, although we are aware that, at that time, there will be malign beings, having no roots of goodness, conceited, fond of gain and honor, rooted in unholiness, difficult to tame, deprived of good will, and really unwilling to learn about the Dharma. In spite of these difficulties, we will read, keep, preach, write, honor, respect, venerate, and worship the Lotus Sutra. We will be willing to sacrifice our body and life, to divulge this Sutra. Let the Lord be at ease. Then five hundred monks of the assembly, including those who were under training and those who were not, said to the Lord, "We also will exert ourselves, enthusiastically, to divulge this Sutra, although we will do so in other worlds." LS Chapter 13

4.49 अथ खलु ता भिक्षुण्यः इमां गाथां भाषित्वा
भगवन्तं एतदूचुः वयमपि भगवन् समुत्सहामहे
इमं धर्मपर्यायं सम्प्रकाशयितुं पश्चिमे काले
पश्चिमे समये अपि तु अन्यासु लोकधातुषु इति ।। LS Chapter 13

atha khalu ta bhiksunyah imam gatham
bhasitva bhagavantam etaducuh vayamapi
bhagavan samutsamahe imam dharmaparyayam
samprakasayitum pascime kale pascime samaye
api tu anyasu lokadhatusu iti —*LS Chapter 13*

Simple meaning—Thousands of nuns too said to the Lord, "We also will exert ourselves, enthusiastically, to divulge the Lotus Sutra, although we will do so in other worlds."

LS Chapter 13

4.50 आक्रोशांस्तर्जनांश्चैव दण्ड उद्गुरणानि च।
बालानां संसहिष्यामः अधिवासिष्याम नायक ।। LS 13.3
अरण्यवृत्तकाश्चैव कन्थां प्रावरियाण च।
संलेखवृत्तिचारी स्म एवं वक्ष्यन्ति दुर्मति ।। LS 13.5
रौद्रचित्ताश्च दुष्टाश्च गृहवित्तविचिन्तकाः।
अरण्यगुप्तिं प्रविशित्वा अस्माकं परिवादकाः ।। LS 13.7
गौरवेणेह लोकेन्द्र उत्सहाम सुदुष्करम्।
क्षान्तीय कक्ष्यां बंधित्वा सूत्रमेतं प्रकाशये ।। LS 13.14

akrosanstarjanamscaiva danda udguranani ca
balanam samsahisyamah adhivasisyama nayaka
—*LS 13.3*

aranyavrittakascaiva kantham pravariyana ca
samlekhavritticari sma evam vaksyanti durmati
—*LS 13.5*

raudracittasca dustasca grihavittavicintakah
aranyaguptim pravisitva asmakam parivadakah
—*LS 13.7*

gauraveneha lokendra utsahama suduskaram
ksantiya kaksyam bandhitva sutrametam prakasaye
—*LS 13.14*

Simple meaning—Eighty hundred thousand Bodhisattvas said to the Lord: We will suffer, patiently endure, the injuries, threats, blows, and attack with sticks, at the hands of ignorant men. LS 13.3

We will be willing to live in the wilderness and wear a patched cloth, we will be willing to live in poverty and listen to the insults of ignorant men. LS 13.5

Cruel-minded and wicked men will enter our retreat in the forest and will try to destroy us. LS 13.7

Since we firmly believe that the bodhisattva-vow must be adhered to, we will do non-violent action under any circumstances. Girded with the girdle of forbearance, we will promulgate the Lotus Sutra. LS 13.14

4.51 इदानीं खलु पुनरहं कुलपुत्रा अपरिनिर्वायमाण एव
परिनिर्वाणमारोचयामि। तत्कस्य हेतोः।
सत्त्वानहं कुलपुत्रा अनेन पर्यायेण परिपाचयामि।
मा हैव मेऽतिचिरं तिष्ठतोऽभीक्ष्णदर्शनेन
अकृतकुशलमूलाः सत्त्वाः पुण्यविरहिता
दरिद्रभूताः कामलोलुपा अन्धा दृष्टिजालसंछन्नाः
तिष्ठति तथागत इति विदित्वा किलीकृतसंज्ञा
भवेयुः, न च तथागते दुर्लभसंज्ञामुत्पादयेयुः
आसन्ना वयं तथागतस्येति। वीर्यं नारभेयुः
त्रैधातुकान् निःसरणार्थं न च तथागते
दुर्लभसंज्ञामुत्पादयेयुः। ततः कुलपुत्राः तथागतः
उपायकौशल्येन तेषां सत्त्वानां दुर्लभप्रादुर्भावो
भिक्षवस्तथागत इति वाचं व्याहरति स्म ॥ LS Chapter 16

idanim khalu punaraham kulaputra aparinirvayamana eva parinirvanamarocayami tatkasya hetoh sattvanaham kulaputra anena paryanena paripacayami. ma haiva me'ticiram tisthato' bhiksnadarsanena akritakusalamulah sattvah punyavirahita daridrabhutah

kamalolupa andha dristijalasamchannah
tisthati tathagata iti viditva kilikritasamjna
bhaveyuh, na ca tathagate durlabhasamjnam-
-utpadayeyuh asanna vayam tathagatasyeti
viryam narabheyuh traidhatukan nihsaranartham
na ca tathagate durlabhasamjnamutpadayeyuh
tatah kulaputrah tathagatah upayakausalyena
tesam sattvanam durlabhapradurbhavo
bhiksavastathagata iti vacam vyaharati sma.

—LS Chapter 16

Simple meaning—The Lord said : I announce final extinction, young men of good family, although I do not become finally extinct. For in this way, I bring all beings to maturity; otherwise those people, in whom goodness is not firmly rooted, who are unholy, miserable, attached to worldly pleasures, spiritually blind, deluded by wrong vision, might think: "The Tathagata is not going to disappear–we see him all the time." And because of such thinking, they might become lazy and inactive–and by failing to put in the right effort, they might not be able to free themselves from the samsara. Due to this type of thinking, people do not realize how precious Tathagata's presence is. Hence, young men of good family, the Tathagata makes use of his skilfulness and declares: Consider yourself lucky that you are able to see the Tathagata. LS Chapter 16

4.52 पुनश्च क्षान्ति भावेत दांतभूमौ प्रतिष्ठितः।
धृतिमान् स्मृतिमांश्चैव परिभाषाः क्षमे बहुः ।। LS 17.23
ये चोपलम्भिकाः सत्त्वा अधिमाने प्रतिष्ठिताः।
कुत्सनं च सहेत्तेषां बुद्धज्ञानस्य कारणात् ।। LS 17.24
अरण्यवासी तिष्ठन्तो चंक्रमं अभिरुह्य च।
स्त्यानमिद्धं च वर्जित्वा कल्पकोट्यो हि यश्चरेत् ।। LS 17.26
तेन ध्यानेन सो वीरः प्रार्थयेद् बोधिमुत्तमाम्।
अहं स्यामिति सर्वज्ञो ध्यानपारमितां गतः ।। LS 17.28

punasca ksanti bhaveta dantabhumau pratisthitah
dhritiman smritimamscaiva paribhasah ksame bahuh
—LS 17.23

ye copalambhikah sattva adhimane pratisthitah
kutsanam ca sahettesam buddhajnanasya karanat
—LS 17.24

aranyavasi tisthanto cankramam abhiruhya ca
styanamiddham ca varjitva kalpakotyo hi yascaret
—LS 17.26

tena dhyanena so virah prarthayed bodhimuttamam
aham syamiti sarvajno dhyanaparamitam gatah
—LS 17.28

Simple meaning—The Lord said that a preacher of Dharma should do the following:-

He should develop the virtue of forbearance, he should be polite, he should have a good memory, he should patiently endure many censures, and should never give up the effort. LS 17.23

He should be aware that non-believers, rooted in pride, usually speak contemptuous words, but still he should not lose heart. LS 17.24

He should be mentally prepared to work under difficult living conditions – be this a part of living in the forest or as a wanderer – but under all circumstances, he should avoid sloth and torpor. LS 17.26

He should have a firm determination to do his duty with a brave heart, and his meditation should be directed to give him strength and to keep him steady in the pursuit of the path that he has chosen. LS 17.28

4.53 Chapter 18 has a long narration to convey the message that the success of a preacher of Dharma lies, not in isolated effort, but in organizing a chain of volunteers.

अथ खलु भगवान् मैत्रेयं बोधिसत्त्वं महासत्त्वं एतदवोचत्
कश्चिदजित कुलपुत्रो वा कुलदुहिता वा तथागतस्य
परिनिर्वृतस्य इमं धर्मपर्यायं देश्यमानं
सम्प्रकाश्यमानं श्रृणुयाद् भिक्षुर्वा भिक्षुणी वा
उपासको वा उपासिका वा विज्ञपुरुषो वा कुमारको
वा कुमारिका वा श्रुत्वा च अभ्यनुमोदेत सचेत्ततो
धर्मश्रवणादुत्थाय प्रक्रामेत् स च विहारगतो वा
गृहगतो वा अरण्यगतो वा वीथिगतो वा
ग्रामगतो वा जनपदगतो वा तान् हेतुंस्तानि
कारणानि तं धर्मं यथाश्रुतम् यथोद्गृहीतम्
यथाबलम् अपरस्य सत्त्वस्याचक्षीत मातुर्वा पितुर्वा
ज्ञातेर्वा सम्मोदितस्य वा अन्यस्य वा संस्तुतस्य
कश्यचित् सोऽपि यदि श्रुत्वा अनुमोदेत अनुमोद्य च
पुनरन्यस्मै आचक्षीत सोऽपि यदि श्रुत्वा अनुमोदेत
अनुमोद्य च सोऽप्यपरस्मै आचक्षीत सोऽपि तं
श्रुत्वा अनुमोदेत इत्यनेन पर्यायेण यावत् पंचाशत्
परम्परया अथ खलु अजित योऽसौ पंचाशत्तमः
पुरुषो भवेत् परम्पराश्रवानुमोदकः तस्यापि
तावदहमजित कुलपुत्रस्य वा कुलदुहितुर्वा
अनुमोदनासहगतं पुण्याभिसंस्कारं अभिनिर्देक्ष्यामि।। LS Chapter 18

atha khalu bhagavan maitreyam bodhisattvam mahasattvam etadavocat kascidajita kulaputro va kuladuhita va tathagatasya parinirvritasya imam dharmaparyayam desyamanam samprakasyamanam srinuyad bhiksurva bhiksuni va upasako va upasika va vijnapuruso va kumarako va kumarika va srutva ca abhyanvmodeta sacettato dharmasravanadutthaya prakramet sa ca viharagato va grihagato va aranyagato va vithigato va gramagato va janapadagato va tan hetumstani karanani tam dharmam yathasrutam yathodgrihitam yathabalam aparasya sattvasyacaksita

maturva piturva jnaterva sammoditasya
va anyasya va samstutasya kasyacit so'pi
yadi srutva anumodeta anumodya ca
punaranyasmai acaksita so'pi yadi srutva
anumodeta anumodya ca so'pyaparasmai
acaksita so'pi tam srutva anumodeta ityanena
paryayena yavat pancasat paramparaya atha
khalu ajita yo'sau pancasattamah puruso
bhavet paramparasravanumodakah tasyapi
tavadahamajita kulaputrasya va kuladuhiturva
anumodanasahagatam punyabhisamskaram
abhinirdeksyami *LS Chapter 18*

Simple meaning—The Lord said to the Bodhisattva Mahasattva Maitreya: If any one, Ajita, either a young man of good family or a young woman, after the complete extinction of the Tathagata, hears the preaching of the Lotus Sutra, let it be a monk or nun, a male or female lay devotee, a man of ripe understanding or a boy or girl; if the hearer joyfully accepts it, and then rises up to go elsewhere, to a monastery, house, forest, street, village, town, or province, with the motive and express aim to expound the dharma, such as he has understood, such as he has heard it, and according to his capability, to another person, his mother, father, kinsman, friend, acquaintance, or any other person; if the latter, after hearing, joyfully accepts, and, in consequence, communicates it to another, if the latter, after hearing, joyfully accepts, and communicates it to another; if this other, again, after hearing, joyfully accepts it, and so on in succession until a number of fifty is reached; then, Ajita, the fiftieth person to hear and joyfully accept the dharma so heard, let it be a young man of good family or a young woman, will have acquired an accumulation of merit connected with the joyful acceptance, which I am going to indicate.

LS Chapter 18

4.54 Although the main message of Chapter 25 is related to 'worship and prayer', a message related to 'non-violent approach' is contained in the following verse :

सचि शत्रुगणैः परिवृतः
शस्त्रहस्तैर्विहिंसचेतसैः।
स्मरतो अवलोकितेश्वरम्
मैत्रचित्त तदा भोंति तत्क्षणम् ।। LS 25.9

saci satruganaih parivritah
sastrahastairvihimsacetasaih
smarato avalokitesvaram
maitracitta tada bhonti tatksanam // *LS 25.9*

Simple meaning—If a man be surrounded by a host of enemies armed with weapons – and the enemies have the intention of killing him – he has but to think of Avalokitesvara, and the enemies will instantaneously become kind-hearted.

LS 25.9

Non-violent action and perservance: Selections from Bodhicaryavatara.

4.55 यदा कुशलयोग्योऽपि कुशलं न करोम्यहम्।
अपायदुःखैः सम्मूढः किं करिष्याम्यहम् तदा ।। BCA 4.18

yada kusalayogyo'pi kusalam na karomyaham
apayaduhkhaih sammudhah kim karisyamyaham tada
—BCA 4.18

Simple meaning—If I do not do good when I am capable of performing my duty, what will I do when I am stupefied by the sorrows arising out of helplessness? BCA 4.18

4.56 अकुर्वतश्च कुशलं पापं चाप्युपचिन्वतः।
हतः सुगतिशब्दोऽपि कल्पकोटिशतैरपि ।। BCA 4.19
अत एवाह भगवान् मानुष्यं अतिदुर्लभम्।
महार्णवयुगच्छिद्रकूर्मग्रीवार्पणोपमम् ।। BCA 4.20

akurvatasca kusalam papam capyupacinvatah
hatah sugatisabdo'pi kalpakotisatairapi *—BCA 4.19*
ata evaha bhagavan manusyam atidurlabham
maharnavayugacchidrakurmagrivarpanopamam
—BCA 4.20

Simple meaning—If we do not perform good actions, and, in stead of that, accumulate evil, the very idea of having obtained a big opportunity in this world, is destroyed for hundreds of millions of years. BCA 4.19

Therefore the Blessed One wanted us to remember always that human life is exceedingly hard to obtain; it is as hard as the possibility that a turtle will ever be able to insert his neck into the cleft of a yoke in the great sea. BCA 4.20

4.57 नातः परा वंचनास्ति न च मोहोऽस्त्यतः परः ।
यदीदृशं क्षणं प्राप्य नाभ्यस्तं कुशलं मया ।। BCA 4.23
यदि चैवं विमृष्यामि पुनः सीदामि मोहितः
शोचिष्यामि चिरं भूयो यमदूतैः प्रचोदितः ।। BCA 4.24

natah para vancanasti na ca moho' styatah parah
yadidrisam ksanam prapya nabhyastam kusalam maya
—BCA 4.23

yadi caivam vimrisyami punah sidami mohitah
socisyami ciram bhuyo yamadutaih pracoditah
—BCA 4.24

Simple meaning—Having obtained a brief moment which is endowed with such opportunities, there is certainly no greater deception and no greater stupidity than not applying myself to goodness. BCA 4.23

And if, indeed, I am again distressed and I sit stupidly inactive, once more I shall burn for a long while as I am driven on by the messengers of death. BCA 4.24

4.58 सर्वे हिताय कल्पन्ते आनुकूल्येन सेविताः ।
सेव्यमानास्त्वमी क्लेशाः सुतरां दुःखकारकाः ।। BCA 4.33

sarve hitaya kalpante anukulyena sevitah
sevyamanastvami klesah sutaram duhkhakarakah
—BCA 4.33

Simple meaning—All could be turned to advantage if favorable opportunities of service are not allowed to be lost. On the other hand, if difficulties are allowed to make you inactive, then they become even more the creators of sorrow. BCA 4.33

4.59 स्वजीविकामात्रनिबद्धचित्ताः
कैवर्तचण्डालकृषीवलाद्यः।
शीतातपादिव्यसनं सहन्ते
जगद्धितार्थं न कथं सहेऽहम् ।। BCA 4.40

svajivikamatranibaddhacittah
kaivartacandalakrisivaladyah
sitatapadivyasanam sahante
jagaddhitartham na katham sahe'ham —BCA 4.40

Simple meaning—With their minds fixed upon earning a livelihood, fishermen, outcastes, farmers, and the like, prevail over the misfortunes of cold, heat, and similar difficulties. Why shall I not prevail over my difficulties, in the work of the world's well-being? BCA 4.40

4.60 सुखार्थं क्रियते कर्म तथापि स्यान्न वा सुखम्।
कर्मैव तु सुखं यस्य निष्कर्मा स सुखी कथम् ।। BCA 7.63

sukhartham kriyate karma tathapi syanna va sukham
karmaiva tu sukham yasya niskarma sa sukhi katham
—BCA 7.63

Simple meaning—How can such a person whose happiness lies in activity, be happy when not active; since, whether or not happiness is the outcome of effort, he can not sit idle. BCA 7.63

The above two verses of Shantideva look like a rephrasing of the following verses of Bhagavad-Gita:-

न हि कश्चित् क्षणमपि जातु तिष्ठत्यकर्मकृत् । BG 3.5
शरीरयात्राऽपि च ते न प्रसिध्येदकर्मणः।। BG 3.8
कर्मणैव हि संसिद्धिं आस्थिता जनकादयः।
लोकसंग्रहमेवापि संपश्यन् कर्तुमर्हसि ।। BG 3.20

na hi kascit ksanamapi jatu tisthatyakarmakrit —*BG 3.5*
sarirayatra'pi ca te na prasidhyedakarmanah —*BG 3.8*
karmanaiva hi samsiddhim asthita janakadayah
lokasamgrahamevapi sampasyan kartumarhasi —*BG 3.20*

Simple meaning—No one can remain even for a moment without doing work. BG 3.5

Even the maintenance of human life is impossible without the performance of work. BG 3.8

In order to determine the right course of action, one has to take into account 'lokasamgraha' (good of the world). Perfect karmayogins like Janaka did this, and this was the key to their greatness. BG 3.20

4.61 सद्धर्मसेवकं कायमितरार्थं न पीडयेत्।
एवमेव हि सत्त्वानां आशामाशु प्रपूरयेत् ।। BCA 5.86
saddharmasevakam kayamitarartham na pidayet
evameva hi sattvanam asamasu prapurayet
—*BCA 5.86*

Simple meaning—One ought not to torture the body, which is the dwelling place of the true Dharma. Only when the body is properly maintained, will it enable the person to perform good deeds efficiently. BCA 5.86

4.62 विश्वस्तविन्यस्तपदं विस्पष्टार्थं मनोरमम्।
श्रुतिसौख्यं कृपामूलं मृदुमन्दस्वरं वदेत् ।। BCA 5.79
visvastavinyastapadam vispastartham manoramam
srutisaukhyam kripamulam mridumandasvaram
vadet —*BCA 5.79*

Simple meaning—One should speak sentences which convey the message clearly, which are pleasing to the mind, gratifying to the ears, filled with compassion, and in a soft and gentle tone. BCA 5.79

4.63 ऋजु पश्येत् सदा सत्त्वान् चक्षुषा सम्पिबन्निव।
एतानेव समाश्रित्य बुद्धत्वं मे भविष्यति ।। BCA 5.80

riju pasyet sada sattvan caksusa sampibanniva
etaneva samasritya buddhatvam me bhavisyati

—*BCA 5.80*

Simple meaning—With the eyes one should look honestly and sincerely at beings, as if they are sharing a soft and pleasant drink. Thus, by establishing mutual regard, every one will achieve Buddhahood. BCA 5.80

4.64 एवं वशीकृतस्वात्मा नित्यं स्मितमुखो भवेत्।
त्यजेद् भृकुटिसंकोचं पूर्वाभाषी जगत्सुहृत् ।। BCA 5.71

evam vasikritasvatma nityam smitamukho bhavet
tyajet bhrikutisankocam purvabhasi jagatsuhrit

—*BCA 5.71*

Simple meaning—Observing self-discipline, one should always have a smiling countenance. One should never have frowns and suspicious looks, one should be the first to introduce oneself, and sincerely be a friend of the world. BCA 5.71

4.65 छन्दस्थामरतिमुक्तिबलं सत्त्वार्थसिद्धये।
छन्दं दुःखभयात् कुर्याद् अनुशंसांश्च भावयन् ।। BCA 7.31

chandasthamaratimuktibalam sattvarthasiddhaye
chandam duhkhabhayat kuryad anusamsamsca
bhavayan —*BCA 7.31*

Simple meaning—For achieving the welfare of beings, one can make use of the power of zeal, constancy, joy, and release. Zeal helps remove the fear of sorrow, and it becomes particularly beneficial because it encourages activism.
BCA 7.31

एवं विपक्षमुन्मूल्य यतेतोत्साहवृद्धये।
छन्दमानरतित्यागतात्पर्यवशिताबलैः ।। BCA 7.32

evam vipaksamunmulya yatetotsahavriddhaye
chandamanaratityagatatparyavasitabalaih—*BCA 7.32*

Simple meaning—Therefore, after having removed the fear of sorrow, one should strive enthusiastically for increase of strength, by means of the power of zeal, pride, joy, sacrifice, dedication, and commitment. BCA 7.32

4.66 दक्ष उत्थानसम्पन्नः स्वयंकारी सदा भवेत्।
नावकाशः प्रदातव्यः कस्यचित् सर्वकर्मसु ।। BCA 5.82

daksa utthanasampannah svayamkari sada bhavet
navakasah pradatavyah kasyacit sarvakarmasu —BCA 5.82

Simple meaning—One should be skilful, endowed with energy, and always self-reliant. There is to be no dependence upon any one in any act. (Co-operation is fine, but no dependence). BCA 5.82

4.67 एवं बुद्ध्वा परार्थेषु भवेत् सततमुत्थितः।
निषिद्धमप्यनुज्ञातं कृपालोरर्थदर्शिनः ।। BCA 5.84

evam buddhva pararthesu bhavet satatamutthitah
nisiddhamapyanujnatam kripalorarthadarsinah
—BCA 5.84

Simple meaning—Thus enlightened, one ought to be constantly active for the sake of others. Even that which is generally forbidden, is allowed to the one who is engaged in the work of compassion. (Reference to upayakausalya of the Lotus Sutra). BCA 5.84

4.68 या अवस्थाः प्रपद्येत स्वयं परवशोऽपि वा।
तास्ववस्थासु याः शिक्षाः शिक्षेत्ता एव यत्नतः ।। BCA 5.99

ya avasthah prapadyeta svayam paravaso'pi va
tasvavasthasu yah siksah siksetta eva yatnatah
—BCA 5.99

Simple meaning—Whatever circumstances one may experience, either caused by oneself or by others, one should zealously practice whatever is most appropriate at that time. (There is an obvious reference to Bhagavad-Gita's message of 'desh-kala-patra' which means 'adjustment to time, place, and circumstances'). BCA 5.99

4.69 न हि तद्विद्यते किंचिद्यन्न शिक्ष्यं जिनात्मजैः।
न तदस्ति न यत्पुण्यं एवं विहरतः सतः ।। BCA 5.100

na hi tadvidyate kincidyanna siksyam jinatmajaih
na tadasti na yatpunyam evam viharatah satah

—BCA 5.100

Simple meaning—Since the Bodhisattvas are so well disciplined, they make proper adjustments under all circumstances. They turn every thing in the right direction, to serve the cause of goodness. BCA 5.100

4.70 मयान्यदुःखं हन्तव्यं दुःखत्वादात्मदुःखवत्।
अनुग्राह्या मयान्येऽपि सत्त्वत्वादात्मसत्त्ववत् ।। BCA 8.94

mayanyaduhkham duhkhatvadatmaduhkhavat
anugrahya mayanye'pi sattvatvadatmasattvavat

—BCA 8.94

Simple meaning—Other people's sorrow is to be destroyed by me because it is sorrow like my own sorrow. Similarly, others are to be honored by me because their self is like my own self. BCA 8.94

There is an obvious reference here to the following verse of Bhagavad-Gita:

आत्मौपम्येन सर्वत्र समं पश्यति योऽर्जुन।
सुखं वा यदि वा दुःखं स योगी परमो मतः ।। BG 6.32

atmaupamyena sarvatra samam pasyati yo'rjuna
sukham va yadi va duhkham sa yogi paramo matah

—BG 6.32

Simple meaning—A spiritually advanced person is guided by the philosophy of seeing the same self in all the beings. Furthermore, this person's sympathetic behavior towards all reflects this philosophy fully, in the sense that he is happy when others are happy and he is unhappy when others are unhappy. BG 6.32

4.71 सर्वमेतत्सुचरितं दानं सुगतपूजनम्।
कृतं कल्पसहस्रैः यत्प्रतिघः प्रतिहन्ति तत् ।। BCA 6.1

sarvametatsucaritam danam sugatapujanam
kritam kalpasahasraih yatpratighah pratihanti tat
—BCA 6.1

Simple meaning—One who sees the same self in all, has to avoid hostility, which destroys all the moral conduct, charity, and reverence of the Buddhas – all that has been achieved in millions of years. BCA 6.1

4.72 न च द्वेषसमं पापं न च क्षान्तिसमं तपः।
तस्मात् क्षान्तिं प्रयत्नेन भावयेद् विविधैर्नयैः ।। BCA 6.2

na ca dvesasamam papam na ca ksantisamam tapah
tasmat ksantim prayatnena bhavayed vividhairnayaih
—BCA 6.2

Simple meaning—One must consider hostility and hatred as the greatest sin, and tolerance and patience as the greatest virtue – and all efforts should be made to cultivate this virtue. BCA 6.2

4.73 मनः शमं न गृह्णाति न प्रीतिसुखमश्नुते।
न निद्रां न धृतिं याति द्वेषशल्ये हृदि स्थिते ।। BCA 6.3

manah samam na grihnati na pritisukhamasnute
na nidram na dhritim yati dvesasalye hridi sthite
—BCA 6.3

Simple meaning—When a person has the arrow of hatred within his heart, he can not achieve a tranquil mind nor attain the joy of harmony, restful sleep and fortitude. BCA 6.3

सुहृदोऽपि उद्विजन्तेऽस्माद् ददाति न च सेव्यते।
संक्षेपान्नास्ति तत् किंचित् क्रोधनो येन सुस्थितः ।। BCA 6.5

suhrido'pi udvijante'smad dadati na ca sevyate
samksepannasti tatkincit krodhano yena susthitah
—BCA 6.5

Simple meaning—Even friends shrink from such a person, and no mutual give-and-take relationship can exist with him. In this way, a person burdened with hatred and anger, closes all doors to happiness. BCA 6.5

4.74 एवमादीनि दुःखानि करोतीत्यरिसंज्ञया ।
यः क्रोधं हन्ति निर्बन्धात् स सुखीह परत्र च ।। BCA 6.6

evamadini duhkhani karotityarisanjnaya
yah krodham hanti nirbandhat sa sukhiha paratra ca
—BCA 6.6

Simple meaning—But a person, who with perseverance destroys anger, and who establishes mutual understanding with the adversary – that one is happy in this world, and in the other world too. BCA 6.6

4.75 अनिष्टकरणाज्जातमिष्टस्य च विघातनात् ।
दौर्मनस्याशनं प्राप्य द्वेषो दृप्तो निहन्ति माम् ।। BCA 6.7
तस्माद् विघातयिष्यामि तस्याशनं अहं रिपोः ।
यस्मान्न मद्वधाद् अन्यत् कृत्यमस्यास्ति वैरिणः ।। BCA 6.8

anistakaranajjatamistasya ca vighatanat
daurmanasyasanam prapya dveso dripto nihanti mam
—BCA 6.7

tasmad vighatayisyami tasyasanam aham ripoh
yasmanna madvadhad anyat krityamasyasti vairinah
—BCA 6.8

Simple meaning—The real factor causing hatred is wrong-doing, and similarly, non-fulfilment of desire is causing anger – but the net result is my unhappiness. BCA 6.7

Therefore, I must destroy the origin or root cause of hatred and anger, that is, wrong-doing and improper desire – because if such remedial action is not done, I cannot put an end to my own unhappiness. BCA 6.8

4.76 दुःखं प्रवेष्टुकामस्य ये कपाटत्वमागताः ।
बुद्धाधिष्ठानत इव द्वेषस्तेषु कथं मम ।। BCA 6.101

duhkham pravestukamasya ye kapatatvamagatah
buddhadhisthanata iva dvesastesu katham mama
—BCA 6.101

Simple meaning—Since I am myself responsible for my unhappiness, I realize that those who appear to cause me suffering, are like Buddhas bestowing their blessings; so why should I get angry with them? BCA 6.101

पुण्यविघ्नः कृतोऽनेनेत्यत्र कोपो न युज्यते।
क्षान्त्या समं तपो नास्ति नन्वेतत्तदुपस्थितम् ।। BCA 6.102
punyavighnah krito' nenetyatra kopo na yujyate
ksantya samam tapo nasti nanvetattadupasthitam
—BCA 6.102

Simple meaning—Blaming others for one's suffering is only an excuse for anger – and this is not the right approach. So control of anger is necessary for one's spiritual progress, and this is facilitated by developing patience. BCA 6.102

अथाहमात्मदोषेण न करोमि क्षमामिह।
मयैवात्र कृतो विघ्नः पुण्यहेतावुपस्थिते ।। BCA 6.103
athahamatmadosena na karomi ksamamiha
mayaivatra krito vighnah punyahetavupasthite
—BCA 6.103

Simple meaning—Considering all this, one must realize that real obstacles in the way of goodness are not caused by any one else, but by oneself. BCA 6.103

Worship and prayer: Selections from Lotus Sutra

4.77 Chapter 25 is the most important chapter dealing with 'worship and prayer'. We start with a part of the prose narration and then present selected verses.

4.78 इह कुलपुत्रा यावन्ति सत्त्वकोटिनयुतशतसहस्राणि
यानि दुःखानि अनुभवन्ति तानि सचेदवलोकितेश्वरस्य
बोधिसत्त्वस्य महासत्त्वस्य नामधेयं शृणुयुः ते सर्वे
तस्माद् दुःखस्कन्धाद् परिमुच्येरन् ।। LS Chapter 25

iha kulaputra yavanti sattvakotinayuta–
–satasahasrani yani duhkhani anubhavanti
tani sacedavalokitesvarasya bodhisattvasya
mahasattvasya namadheyam srinuyuh te sarve
tasmad duhkhaskandhad parimucyeran

—LS Chapter 25

Simple meaning—O young men of good family, all the hundred thousands of millions of beings, who in this world, are suffering from troubles, will, if they hear the name of the Bodhisattva Mahasattva Avalokitesvara, be released from that mass of troubles. LS Chapter 25

4.79 श्रवणोऽथ दर्शनोऽपि च
अनुपूर्वं च तथाऽनुस्मृतिः ।
भवतीहामोघा प्राणिनाम्
सर्वदुःखभवशोकनाशकः ।। LS 25.4

sravano'tha darsano'pi ca
anupurvam ca tatha'nusmritih
bhavatihamogha praninam
sarvaduhkhabhavasokanasakah *—LS 25.4*

Simple meaning—Hearing, seeing, regularly and constantly thinking of Avalokitesvara, will infallibly destroy all suffering, mundane existence, and grief of living beings here on earth. LS 25.4

4.80 सचि अग्निखदाय पातयेद्
घतनार्थाय प्रदुष्टमानसः ।
स्मरतो अवलोकितेश्वरम्
अभिसिक्तो इव अग्नि शामयति ।। LS 25.5

saci agnikhadaya patayed
ghatanarthaya pradustamanasah
smarato avalokitesvaram
abhisikto iva agni samayati *LS 25.5*

Simple meaning—If one be thrown into a pit of fire, by a wicked enemy with the object of killing him, he has but to think of Avalokitesvara, and the fire will be quenched as if sprinkled with water. LS 25.5

4.81 सचि सागरदुर्गि पातयेत्
नागमकरसुरभूत आलये।
स्मरतो अवलोकितेश्वरम्
जलराजे न कदाचि सीदति ।। LS 25.6

saci sagaradurgi patayet
nagamakarasurabhuta alaye
smarato avalokitesvaram
jalaraje na kadaci sidati —*LS 25.6*

Simple meaning—If one happens to fall into the dreadful ocean, the abode of Nagas, marine monsters, and demons, he has but to think of Avalokitesvara, and he will never sink down in the ocean. LS 25.6

4.82 सचि मेरुतलातु पातयेत्
घतनार्थाय प्रदुष्टमानसः।
स्मरतो अवलोकितेश्वरम्
सूर्यभूतो व नभे प्रतिष्ठति ।। LS 25.7

saci merutalatu patayet
ghatanarthaya pradustamanasah
smarato avalokitesvaram
suryabhuto na nabhe pratisthati —*LS 25.7*

Simple meaning—If a man happens to be hurled down from the brink of Mount Meru, by some wicked person with the object of killing him, he has but to think of Avalokitesvara, and he will, sunlike, stand firm in the sky. LS 25.7

4.83 वज्रमय पर्वतो यदि
घतनार्थाय हि मूर्ध्नि ओषरेत्।
स्मरतो अवलोकितेश्वरम्
रोमकूप न प्रभन्ति हिंसितुम् ।। LS 25.8

vajramaya parvato yadi
ghatanarthaya hi murdhni osaret

smarato avalokitesvaram
romakupa na prabhanti himsitum —*LS 25.8*

Simple meaning—If rocks of thunderstorm and thunderbolts are thrown at a man's head to kill him, he has but to think of Avalokitesvara, and they will not be able to hurt one hair of his body. LS 25.8

4.84 सचि शत्रुगणैः परिवृतः
शस्त्रहस्तैर्विहिंसचेतसैः ।
स्मरतो अवलोकितेश्वरम्
मैत्रचित्त तदा भोंति तत्क्षणम् ।। LS 25.9
saci satruganaih parivritah
sastrahastairvihimsacetasaih
smarato avalokitesvaram
maitracitta tada bhonti tatksanam —*LS 25.9*

Simple meaning—If a man be surrounded by a host of enemies armed with weapons – and the enemies have the intention of killing him – he has but to think of Avalokitesvara, and the enemies will instantaneously become kind-hearted. LS 25.9

4.85 सचि आघतने उपस्थितो
वध्यघातनवशंगतो भवेत् ।
स्मरतो अवलोकितेश्वरम्
खण्डखण्ड तत् शस्त्र गच्छियुः ।। LS 25.10
saci aghatane upasthito
vadhyaghatanavasangato bhavet
smarato avalokitesvaram
khandakhanda tat sastra gacchiyuh —*LS 25.10*

Simple meaning—If a man, delivered to executioners, is already standing at the place of execution, he has but to think of Avalokitesvara, and their swords will go to pieces. LS 25.10

4.86 सचि दारुमयैरयोमयैः
हडिनिगडैरिह बद्धबन्धनैः ।

स्मरतो अवलोकितेश्वरम्
क्षिप्रमेव विपटन्ति बन्धनाः ।। LS 25.11

saci darumayairayomayaih
hadinigadairiha baddhabandhanaih
smarato avalokitesvaram
ksiprameva vipatanti bandhanah —*LS 25.11*

Simple meaning—If a man happens to be fettered in shackles of wood or iron, he has but to think of Avalokitesvara, and the bonds will be speedily loosened. LS 25.11

4.87 मंत्र बल विद्य ओषधि
भूत वेताल शरीरनाशकाः ।
स्मरतो अवलोकितेश्वरम्
तान् गच्छन्ति यतः प्रवर्तिताः ।। LS 25.12

mantra bala vidya osadhi
bhuta vetala sariranasakah
smarato avalokitesvaram
tan gacchanti yatah pravartitah —*LS 25.12*

Simple meaning—Mighty spells, witchcraft, herbs, ghosts, and spectres, pernicious to life, revert thither whence they came, when one thinks of Avalokitesvara. LS 25.12

4.88 सचि ओजहरैः परिवृतो
नागयक्षासुरभूतराक्षसैः ।
स्मरतो अवलोकितेश्वरम्
रोमकूप न प्रभन्ति हिंसितुम् ।। LS 25.13

saci ojaharaih parivrito
nagayaksasurabhutaraksasaih
smarato avalokitesvaram
romakupa na prabhanti himsitum —*LS 25.13*

Simple meaning—If a man is surrounded by goblins, Nagas, demons, ghosts, or giants, who take away bodily vigour, he has but to think of Avalokitesvara, and they will not be able to hurt one hair of his body. LS 25.13

4.89 सचि व्यालमृगैः परिवृतः
तीक्ष्णदंष्ट्रनखरैः महाभयैः ।
स्मरतो अवलोकितेश्वरम्
क्षिप्रं गच्छन्ति दिशा अनन्ततः ।। LS 25.14

saci vyalamrigaih parivritah
tiksnadamstranakharaih mahabhayaih
smarato avalokitesvaram
ksipram gacchanti disa anantatah —*LS 25.14*

Simple meaning—If a man is surrounded by fearful beasts with sharp teeth and claws, he has but to think of Avalokitesvara, and they will quickly fly off in all directions. LS 25.14

4.90 सचि दृष्टिविषैः परिवृतो
ज्वलनार्चिशिखिदुष्टदारुणैः ।
स्मरतो अवलोकितेश्वरम्
क्षिप्रमेव ते भवन्ति निर्विषाः ।। LS 25.15

saci dristivisaih parivrito
jvalanarcisikhidustadarunaih
smarato avalokitesvaram
kispram te bhavanti nirvisah —*LS 25.15*

Simple meaning—If a man is surrounded by snakes, malicious and frightful on account of the flames and fires which they emit, he has but to think of Avalokitesvara, and they will quickly lose their poison. LS 25.15

4.91 गम्भीर सविद्यु निश्चरी
मेघवज्राशनि वारिप्रसवैः ।
स्मरतो अवलोकितेश्वरम्
क्षिप्रमेव प्रशमन्ति तत्क्षणम् ।। LS 25.16

gambhira savidyu niscari
meghavajrasani variprasavaih
smarato avalokitesvaram
ksiprameva prasamanti tatksanam —*LS 25.16*

Simple meaning—If a heavy thunderbolt shoots from a cloud with lightning and thunder, one has but to think of

Avalokitesvara, and the fire of the skies will quickly, instantaneously be quenched. LS 25.16

4.92 बहुदुःखशतैरुपद्रुतान्
सत्त्व दृष्ट्वा बहुदुःखपीडितान्।
शुभज्ञानबलो विलोकिय
तेन त्रातरु गजे सदेवके ।। LS 25.17

bahuduhkhasatairupadrutan
sattva dristva bahuduhkhapiditan
subhajnanabalo vilokiya
tena trataru gaje sadevake —*LS 25.17*

Simple meaning—Avalokitesvara with his powerful knowledge, beholds all beings and protects them from all troubles and sorrows – he is a saviour in the world, including the gods. LS 25.17

4.93 ऋद्धिबलपारमिंगतो
विपुलज्ञान उपायशिक्षितः।
सर्वत्र दशद्दिशि जगे
सर्वक्षेत्रेषु अशेष दृश्यते ।। LS 25.18

riddhibalaparamingato
vipulajnana upayasiksitah
sarvatra dasaddisi jage
sarvaksetresu asesa drisyate —*LS 25.18*

Simple meaning—Avalokitesvara can be seen in all directions and in all regions of the world, because he has superhuman powers, and possesses vast knowledge and skilfulness. LS 25.18

Worship and prayer : Selections from Bodhicaryavatara

4.94 ददामि चात्मानमहं जिनेभ्यः
सर्वेण सर्वं च तदात्मजेभ्यः।
परिग्रहं मे कुरुताग्रसत्त्वा
युष्मासु दासत्वमुपैमि भक्त्या ।। BCA 2.8

परिग्रहेणास्मि भवत्कृतेन
निर्भीर्भावे सत्त्वहितं करोमि।
पूर्वं च पापं समतिक्रमामि
नान्यच्च पापं प्रकरोमि भूयः ।। BCA 2.9

dadami catmanamaham jinebhyah
sarvena sarvam ca tadatmajebhyah
parigraham me kurutagrasattva
yusmasu dasatvamupaimi bhaktya —*BCA 2.8*
parigrahenasmi bhavatkritena
nirbhirbhave sattvahitam karomi
purvam ca papam samatikramami
nanyacca papam prakaromi bhuyah —*BCA 2.9*

Simple meaning—I give myself to the Buddhas and the Bodhisattvas, completely. Kindly take possession of me. Through devotion, I go into your servitude. Having surrendered myself to your grace, I have no fear about myself. I confess my former sin, and take the vow to do no further sin. Kindly give me strength to do good to all. BCA 2.8-9

4.95 बुद्धं गच्छामि शरणं यावद् बोधिमण्डतः
धर्मं गच्छामि शरणं बोधिसत्त्वगणं तथा ।। BCA 2.26
विज्ञापयामि सम्बुद्धान् सर्वदिक्षु व्यवस्थितान्।
महाकारुणिकांश्चापि बोधिसत्त्वान् कृतांजलिः ।। BCA 2.27
अनेन मम पुण्येन सर्वसत्त्वा अशेषतः।
विरम्य सर्वपापेभ्यः कुर्वन्तु कुशलं सदा ।। BCA 10.31

buddham gacchami saranam yavad bodhimandatah
dharmam gacchami saranam bodhisattvaganam tatha
—*BCA 2.26*

vijnapayami sambuddhan sarvadiksu vyavasthitan
mahakarunikamscapi bodhisattvan kritanjalih
—*BCA 2.27*

anena mama punyena sarvasattva asesatah
viramya sarvapapebhyah kurvantu kusalam sada
—*BCA 10.31*

Simple meaning—I go to the Buddha for refuge, who leads every one to Enlightenment and Bodhisattvahood. I seek the blessings of the Dharma and of all the Bodhisattvas. With folded hands (i.e. in a prayerful posture), I implore the perfect Buddhas as well as the great compassionate Bodhisattvas, who help beings everywhere and listen to their prayers. My prayer is : May beings everywhere, without exception, follow the Dharma and help one another.

BCA 2.26-27, 10.31

4.96 अद्यैव शरणं यामि जगन्नाथान् महाबलान् ।
जगद्रक्षार्थमुद्युक्तान् सर्वत्रासहरान् जिनान् ।। BCA 2.48
तैश्चाप्यधिगतं धर्मं संसारभयनाशनम् ।
शरणं यामि भावेन बोधिसत्त्वगणं तथा ।। BCA 2.49
सर्वासु दिक्षु यावन्तः कायचित्तव्यथातुराः ।
ते प्राप्नुवन्तु मत्पुण्यैः सुखप्रामोद्यसागरान् ।। BCA 10.2

adyaiva saranam yami jagannathan mahabalan
jagadraksarthamudyuktan sarvatrasaharan jinan
—*BCA 2.48*

taiscapyadhigatam dharmam samsarabhayanasanam
saranam yami bhavena bodhisattvaganam tatha
—*BCA 2.49*

sarvasu diksu yavantah kayacittavyathaturah
te prapnuvantu matpunyaih sukhapramodyasagaran
—*BCA 10.2*

Simple meaning—I go now for refuge to the Buddhas, the Lords laboring for the sake of the earth's protection, the conquerors who dispel all fear.

Likewise I go for refuge to the Dharma which the Buddhas have preached, which consumes the fear of samsara, and I go to all the Bodhisattvas. My prayer is : Let all the beings, who are suffering pain of body or of thought, obtain oceans of happiness and joy. BCA 2.48-49, 10.2

4.97 सर्वासु दिक्षु सम्बुद्धान् प्रार्थयामि कृतांजलिः ।
धर्मप्रदीपं कुर्वन्तु मोहाद् दुःखप्रपातिनाम् ।। BCA 3.4

sarvasu diksu sambuddhan prarthayami kritanjalih
dharmapradipam kurvantu mohad duhkhaprapatinam
—BCA 3.4

Simple meaning—With folded hands, I pray to the perfect Buddhas in all places. May they cause the light of the Dharma to shine upon those who, because of ignorance, have fallen into sorrow. BCA 3.4

4.98 आराधनायाद्य तथागतानाम्
सर्वात्मना दास्यमुपैमि लोके ।
कुर्वन्तु मे मूर्ध्नि पदं जनौघा
विघ्नन्तु वा तुष्यतु लोकनाथाः ।। BCA 6.125
तथागताराधनमेतदेव
स्वार्थस्य संसाधनमेतदेव
लोकस्य दुःखापहमेतदेव
तस्मान् ममास्तु व्रतमेतदेव ।। BCA 6.127

aradhanayadya tathagatanam
sarvatmana dasyamupaimi loke
kurvantu me murdhni padam janaugha
vighnantu va tusyatu lokanathah *—BCA 6.125*
tathagataradhanametadeva
svarthasya samsadhanametadeva
lokasya duhkhapahametadeva
tasman mamastu vratametadeva *—BCA 6.127*

Simple meaning—For homage and worship of the Buddhas, I go now with my entire self, to serve the world, Whether people put their feet upon my head or even slay me – I am not concerned about that. May the Lord of the world accept my worship. For achieving the goal of "welfare of all," my immediate contribution is that I take a firm vow, viz. that I will try to destroy the sorrows of the world. I will view this as my worship of the Buddha, and the source of my own happiness too. BCA 6.125, 127

4.99 बोधिसत्त्वमहापर्षन्मण्डलानि समन्ततः।
निषीदन्तु स्वशोभाभिर्मण्डयन्तु महीतलम् ।। BCA 10.36
मा कश्चिद् दुःखितः सत्त्वो मा पापी मा च रोगितः।
मा हीनः परिभूतो वा मा भूतकश्चिच्च दुर्मनाः।। BCA 10.41

bodhisattvamahaparsanmandalani samantatah
nisidantu svasobhabhirmandayantu mahitalam
—BCA 10.36

ma kascid duhkhitah sattvo ma papi ma ca rogitah
ma hinah paribhuto va ma bhutakascicca durmanah
—BCA 10.41

Simple meaning—May groups of Bodhisattvas in great assemblies sit in all places and listen to people's prayers. May the Bodhisattvas adorn the surface of the earth with their splendour. As a result of this, may no being whosoever be unhappy, sinful, sick, forsaken, or despised, and none whosoever feel depressed or melancholy. BCA 10.36, 41

4.100 यत् किंचित् जगतो दुःखं तत् सर्वं मयि पच्यताम्।
बोधिसत्त्वशुभैः सर्वैः जगत् सुखितमस्तु च ।। BCA 10.56

yat kincit jagato duhkham tat sarvam mayi pacyatam
bodhisattvasubhaih sarvaih jagat sukhitamastu ca
—BCA 10.56

Simple meaning—Whatever the sorrow of the world, may all that be absorbed by me; and may the world be comforted by all of the glorious Bodhisattvas. BCA 10.56

4.101 वस्त्रभोजनपानीयं स्रक्चन्दनविभूषणम्।
मनोभिलषितं सर्वं लभन्तां हितसंहितम् ।। BCA 10.20

vastrabhojanapaniyam srakcandanavibhusanam
manobhilasitam sarvam labhantam hitasamhitam
—BCA 10.20

Simple meaning—May all the people in the world have clothes, food and drink, garlands, sandalwood fragrance, ornaments, all that their heart desires, and all that is most advantageous to them. BCA 10.20

4.102 शीतार्ताः प्राप्नुवन्तूष्णं उष्णार्ताः सन्तु शीतलाः ।
बोधिसत्त्वमहामेघसंभवैः जलसागरैः ।। BCA 10.5

sitartah prapnuvantusnam usnartah santu sitalah
bodhisattvamahameghasambhavaih jalasagaraih
—BCA 10.5

Simple meaning—May those who suffer from cold obtain heat, and may those who suffer from heat be cooled by the rains produced by the great Bodhisattva–clouds. BCA 10.5

आरोग्यं रोगिणामस्तु मुच्यन्तां सर्वबन्धनात् ।
दुर्बला बलिनः सन्तु स्निग्धचित्ताः परस्परम् ।। BCA 10.22

arogyam roginamastu mucyantam sarvabandhanat
durbala balinah santu snigdhacittah parasparam
—BCA 10.22

Simple meaning—May sick people regain health; may all be freed from bondage; may weak people become strong. May all entertain mutually affectionate thoughts and help one another. BCA 10.22

इति मत्कुशलैः समन्तभद्र–
प्रमुखानावृतबोधिसत्त्वमेघान् ।
सुखशीतसुगंधवातवृष्टिम्
अभिनन्दन्तु विलोक्य नारकास्ते ।। BCA 10.15

iti matkusalaih samantabhadra-
pramukhanavritabodhisattvameghan
sukhasitasugandhavatavristim
abhinandantu vilokya narakaste *—BCA 10.15*

Simple meaning—May those in hell welcome the appearance of Bodhisattva-clouds; may they all be freed from hindrance, by the grace of Samantabhadra; may they all feel refreshed by joyful, cool, sweet-smelling rains. BCA 10.15

4.103 भीताश्च निर्भयाः सन्तु शोकार्ताः प्रीतिलाभिनः ।
उद्विग्नाश्च निरुद्वेगा धृतिमन्तो भवन्तु च ।। BCA 10.21

bhitasca nirbhayah santu sokartah pritilabhinah
udvignasca nirudvega dhritimanto bhavantu ca
—BCA 10.21

Simple meaning—May those who are afraid (that they will be punished) get a message of pardon and reform. May those afflicted with sorrow be the obtainers of joy. May those distressed be without distress, and at peace. BCA 10.21

Meditation and dedication: Selections from Lotus Sutra

4.104 चत्वारि धर्मा इमि एवरूपा:
मयि निर्वृते ये च निषेवितव्या: ।
ये चार्थिका उत्तममग्रबोधौ
व्यापारणं ये च कुर्वन्ति मह्यम् ।। LS 14.55
पुनश्च सो पश्यति आत्मभावम्
भावेत धर्मं गिरिकन्दरेषु
भावित्व धर्मं च स्पृशित्व धर्मताम्
समाधि सो लब्धु जिनं च पश्यति ।। LS 14.67
बोधिं च प्राप्तस्ततु व्यूथहित्वा
प्रवर्तयी चक्रमानास्रवं हि ।
चतुर्ण पर्षाण स धर्म देशयी
अचिन्तिया कल्पसहस्रकोट्य: ।। LS 14.71

catvari dharma imi evarupah
mayi nirvrite ye ca nisevitavyah
ye carthika uttamamagrabodhau
vyaparanam ye ca kurvanti mahyam —LS 14.55
punasca so pasyati atmabhavam
bhaveta dharmam girikandaresu
bhavitva dharmam ca sprisitva dharmatam
samadhi so labdhu jinam ca pasyati —LS 14.67
bodhim ca praptastatu vyuthahitva
pravartayi cakramanasravam hi
caturna parsana sa dharma desayi
acintiya kalpasahasrakotyah —LS 14.71

Simple meaning—The Lord said: There are four qualities to be acquired by those who, at the time after my extinction, desire supreme enlightenment, and would like to perform my charge i.e. preach the Lotus Sutra. LS 14.55

The aspirant sees his own self, while engaged in meditation in mountain caverns; and by such meditation, he attains the true nature of the dharma, and, on obtaining complete absorption, sees the Buddha. LS. 14.67

On having reached enlightenment, he will rise up from that place to move forward the faultless wheel and preach the dharma for an inconceivable number of millions of years. LS 14.71

4.105 यश्च पारमिताः पंच समादायेह वर्तते।
इदं ज्ञानं गवेषन्तो बुद्धज्ञानमनुत्तरम् ।। LS 17.17
यश्च ध्यायी महाध्यायी ध्यानारामः समाहितः।
कल्पकोट्यः स्थितो ध्यायेत् सहस्राण्यष्टनूनकाः ।। LS 17.27
तेन ध्यायेन सो वीरः प्रार्थयेद् बोधिमुत्तमाम्।
अहं स्यामिति सर्वज्ञो ध्यानपारमितां गतः ।। LS 17.28

yasca paramitah panca samadayeha vartate
idam jnanam gavesanto buddhajnanamanuttaram
—LS 17.17

yasca dhyayi mahadhyayi dhyanaramah samahitah
kalpakotyah sthito dhyayet sahasranyastanunakah
—LS 17.27

tena dhyayena so virah prarthayed bodhimuttamam
aham syamiti sarvajno dhyanaparamitam gatah
—LS 17.28

Simple meaning—The Lord said : Let a man who is seeking after this knowledge, the superior Buddha-knowledge, undertake to practice in this world, five perfect virtues (including meditation). LS 17.17

Let him as a philosopher, a great philosopher, who finds his delight in meditation, in concentration of mind, pass eight thousand millions of years. LS 17.27

He should have a firm determination to do his duty with a brave heart, and his meditation should be directed to give him strength and to keep him steady in the pursuit of the path that he has chosen. LS 17.28

4.106 Chapter 24 has a long prose-narration relating to 'Meditation'. Furthermore, this chapter has a prose-narration relating to 'Dedication' also. First, we give the narration relating to 'Meditation'. (For the narration on 'Dedication', see para 4.110).

अथ खलु पद्मश्रीः बोधिसत्त्वो महासत्त्वो भगवन्तं
एतदवोचत् अवरोपितकुशलमूलोऽयं भगवन्
गद्गदस्वरो बोधिसत्त्वो महासत्त्वः कतम एष भगवन्
समाधिर्यस्मिन् समाधौ अवस्थितेन गद्गदस्वरेण
बोधिसत्त्वेन महासत्त्वेन इयन्तः सत्त्वा विनीता इति
एवमुक्ते भगवान् शाक्यमुनिस्तथागतोऽर्हन्
सम्यक्सम्बुद्धः पद्मश्रियं बोधिसत्त्वं महासत्त्वं
एतदवोचत् एष हि कुलपुत्र सर्वरूपसंदर्शनो नाम
समाधिः। अस्मिन् समाधौ अवस्थितेन गद्गदस्वरेण
बोधिसत्त्वेन महासत्त्वेन एवं अप्रमेयः सत्त्वार्थः कृतः।
अस्मिन् खलु पुनर्गद्गदस्वरपरिवर्ते निर्दिश्यमाने
यानि गद्गदस्वरेण बोधिसत्त्वेन महासत्त्वेन सार्धं
चतुरशीतिबोधिसत्त्वकोटीनयुतशतसहस्राणि
इमां सहां लोकधातुमागतानि सर्वेषां तेषां
सर्वरूपसंदर्शनस्य समाधेः प्रतिलम्भोऽभूत्।
अस्यां च सहायां लोकधातौ गणनासमतिक्रान्तानां
बोधिसत्त्वानां महासत्त्वानां येषां सर्वरूपसंदर्शनस्य
समाधेः प्रतिलम्भोऽभूत्। ----। सर्वेषां च तेषां
चतुरशीतिबोधिसत्त्वकोटीनयुतशतसहस्राणां
सर्वरूपसंदर्शनस्य समाधेः प्रतिलम्भोऽभूत् ।। LS Chapter 24

atha khalu padmasrih bodhisattvo mahasattvo bhagavantam etadavocat avaropitakusalamulo' yam bhagavan gadgadasvaro bodhisattvo mahasattvah katama esa bhagavam samadhiryasmin samadhau

avasthitena gadgadasvarena bodhisattvena
mahasattvena iyantah sattva vinita iti evamukte
bhagavan sakyamunistathagato'rhan samyaksambuddhah
padmasriyam bodhisattvam mahasattvam etadavocat
esa hi kulaputra sarvarupasandarsano nama samadhih asmin
samadhau avasthitena
gadgadasvarena bodhisattvena mahasattvena evam
aprameyah sattvarthah kritah asmin khalu
punargadgadasvaraparivarte nirdisyamane yani gadgadasvarena
bodhisattvena mahasattvena
sardham caturasitibodhisattvakotinayutasatasahasrani
imam saham lokadhatumagatani sarvesam tesam
sarvarupasandarsanasya samadheh pratilambho' bhut
asyam ca sahayam lokadhatau gananasamatikrantanam
bodhisattvanam mahasattvanam yesam sarvarupasandarsanasya
samadheh pratilambho'bhut ..... sarvesam ca tesam
caturasitibodhisattvakotinayutasatasahasranam
sarvarupasandarsanasya samadheh pratilambho' bhut

—*LS Chapter 24*

Simple meaning—Bodhisattva Mahasattva Padmasri said to the Lord: We have seen that Bodhisattva Mahasattva Gadgadasvara has achieved great success. What meditation is it whereby Bodhisattva Mahasattva Gadgadasvara, with unshaken firmness, has educated so many beings? Then Shakyamuni replied to Bodhisattva Padmasri : It is the meditation named "Sarvarupasandarsana". By steadiness in it has Bodhisattva Gadgadasvara so immensely promoted the welfare of beings. As a follow-up of this, millions of Bodhisattvas, along with Bodhisattva Gadgadasvara, obtained the meditation sarvarupasandarsana, and many more Bodhisattvas did the same....The Chapter concludes by saying that more and more of the Bodhisattvas obtained the meditation named "Sarvarupasandarsana". LS Chapter 24

4.107 In the above narration of Chapter 24, the meditation called 'Sarvarupasandarsana' has been glorified. Chapter 27 goes a step further – it narrates the glory of eight forms of meditation.

तस्य खलु पुनः कुलपुत्रा राज्ञः शुभव्यूहस्य विमलदत्ता
नाम भार्याभूत्। तस्य खलु पुनः कुलपुत्रा राज्ञः
शुभव्यूहस्य द्वौ पुत्रावभूतां एको विमलगर्भो नाम
द्वितीयो विमलनेत्रो नाम। तौ च द्वौ दारकावृद्धिमन्तौ
चाभूतां प्रज्ञावन्तौ च पुण्यवन्तौ च ज्ञानवन्तौ च
बोधिसत्त्वचर्यायां च अभिव्यक्तावभूताम्। तद्यथा-
दानपारमितायामभियुक्तावभूतां शीलपारमितायां
क्षान्तिपारमितायां वीर्यपारमितायां ध्यानपारमितायां
प्रज्ञापारमितायां उपायकौशल्यपारमितायां मैत्र्यां
करुणायां मुदितायां उपेक्षायां यावत् सप्तत्रिंशत्सु
बोधिपक्षिकेषु धर्मेषु। सर्वत्र पारंगतावभूतां
विमलस्य समाधेः पारंगतौ नक्षत्रराजादित्यस्य
समाधेः पारंगतौ विमलनिर्भासस्य समाधेः
पारंगतौ विमलभासस्य समाधेः पारंगतौ
अलंकारशुभस्य समाधेः पारंगतौ महातेजोगर्भस्य
समाधेः पारंगतावभूताम्। ---। विमलनेत्रश्च
दारकोऽस्मिन् धर्मपर्याये चरितावी। विमलगर्भश्च
दारको बहुकल्पकोटीनयुतशतसहस्राणि
सर्वसत्त्वपापजहने समाधौ चरितोऽभूत् किमिति
सर्वसत्त्वाः सर्वपापं जहेयुः इति। ---। प्रव्रजित्वा च
राजा शुभव्यूहः सपरिवारः चतुरशीतिवर्षसहस्राणि
अभियुक्तो विजहार इमं सद्धर्मपुण्डरीकं धर्मपर्यायं
चिन्तयन् भावयन् पर्यवदापयन्। अथ खलु कुलपुत्राः
स राजा शुभव्यूहः तेषां चतुरशीतीनां
वर्षसहस्राणामत्ययेन सर्वगुणालंकारव्यूहं नाम
समाधिं प्रतिलभते स्म। सहप्रतिलब्धाच्चास्य
समाधेः अथ तावदेव सप्ततालमात्रं
वैहायसमभ्युद्गच्छति स्म ।। LS Chapter 27

tasya khalu punah kulaputra rajnah subhavyuhasya vimaladatta nama bharyabhut tasya khalu punah kulaputra rajnah subhavyuhasya dvau putravabhutam eko vimalagarbho nama dvitiyo

vimalanetro nama tau ca dvau dvaraka-
-buddhimantau cabhutam prajnavantau ca
punyavantau ca jnanavantau ca bodhisattva-
-caryayam ca abhivyaktavabhutam tadyatha-
danaparamitayamabhiyuktavabhutam
silaparamitayam ksantiparamitayam
viryaparamitayam dhyanaparamitayam
prajnaparamitayam upayakausalyaparamitayam
maitryam karunayam muditayam upeksayam
yavat saptatrimsatsu bodhipaksikesu dharmesu
sarvatra parangatavabhutam vimalasya samadheh
parangatau naksatrarajadityasya samadheh
parangatau vimalanirbhasasya samadheh
parangatau vimalabhasasya samadheh parangatau
alankarasubhasya samadheh parangatau
mahatejogarbhasya samadheh parangatavabhutam...
...vimalanetrasca darako'smin dharmaparyaye
caritavi vimalagarbhasca dvarako
bahukalpakotinayutasatasahasrani sarvasattva-
-papajahane samadhau carito'bhut kimiti
sarvasattvah sarvapapam jaheyuh iti ....
.... pravrajitva ca raja subhavyuhah saparivarah
caturasitivarsasahasrani abhiyukto vijahara imam
saddharmapundarikam dharmaparyayam cintayan
bhavayan paryavadapayan atha khalu kulaputrah
sa raja subhavyuhah tesam caturasitinam
varsasahasranamatyayena sarvagunalankara-
-vyuham nama samadhi pratilabhate sma
sahapratilabdhaccasya samadheh atha
tavadeva saptatalamatram
vaihayasamabhyudgacchati sma —*LS Chapter 27*

Simple meaning—King Subhavyuha, young men of good family, had a wife named Vimaladatta, and two sons, one named Vimalagarbha, and the other named Vimalanetra. These two boys, who possessed magical power and wisdom, applied themselves to the course of duty of Bodhisattvas, viz. to the perfect virtues (Paramitas) of almsgiving, morality, forbearance, energy, meditation, wisdom, and skilfulness. They were accomplished in benevolence, compassion, joyful sympathy and impartiality, and in all the thirty-seven constituents of true knowledge. They had perfectly mastered six forms of meditation, viz. (i) Meditation Vimala, (ii) Meditation Naksatrarajaditya, (iii) Meditation Vimalanirbhasa, (iv) Meditation Vimalabhasa, (v) Meditation Alankarasura, and (vi) Meditation Mahatejogarbha .... Vimalanetra exercised himself in this Dharmaparyaya (i.e. Lotus Sutra), whereas Vimalagarbha practiced, for millions of years, the seventh form of meditation, viz. (vii) Meditation Sarvasattvapapajahana, with the object that all beings should abandon all evils .... Having become an ascetic, king Subhavyuha, with his retinue, remained for eighty-four thousand years, applying himself to studying, meditating, and thoroughly penetrating this Dharmaparyaya. At the end of those eighty-four thousand years, young men of good family, the King acquired the eighth form of meditation, viz. (viii) meditation Sarvagunalankaravyuha. No sooner had he acquired this meditation, than he rose high up in the sky.

LS Chapter 27

4.108 The Lotus Sutra gives several instances of "Dedication" – out of them we shall present here only three (from Chapters 13, 22, and 24)

अथ खलु भगवान् येन तान्यशीतिबोधिसत्त्वकोटीनयुत-
-शतसहस्राणि धारणीप्रतिलब्धानां बोधिसत्त्वानाम-
-वैवर्तिकधर्मचक्रप्रवर्तकानां तेनावलोकयामास ...
अथ खलु ते कुलपुत्रा भगवतो गौरवेण आत्मनश्च
पूर्वचर्याप्रणिधानेन भगवतोऽभिमुखं सिंहनादं नदन्ते
स्म वयं भगवन् अनागतेऽध्वनि इमं धर्मपर्यायं
तथागते परिनिर्वृते दशसु दिक्षु गत्वा सर्वसत्त्वार्थं
लेखयिष्यामः पाठयिष्यामः चिन्तापयिष्यामः
प्रकाशयिष्यामो भगवत एवानुभावेन ।। LS Chapter 13

atha khalu bhagavan yena tanyasitibodhisattva-
-kotinayutasatasahasrani dharanipratilabdhanam

bodhisattvanamavaivartikadharmacakrapravartakanam tenavalokayamasa .... atha khalu te kulaputra bhagavato gauravena atmanasca purvacarya--pranidhanena bhagavato' bhimukham simhanadam nadante sma vayam bhagavan anagate' dhvani imam dharmaparyayam tathagate parinirvrite dasasu diksu gatva sarvasattvartham lekhayisyamah pathayisyamah cintapayisyamah prakasayisyamo bhagavata evanubhavena

—*LS Chapter 13*

Simple meaning—The Lord looked towards the eighty hundred thousand Bodhisattvas who were gifted with magical spells and were capable of moving forward the wheel of Dharma that never rolls back.... Thereupon all those Bodhisattvas, in consequence of their reverence for the Lord and their own pious vow and dedication, raised a lion's roar and declared before the Lord : We will, in future, after the departure of the Lord, go in all directions, in order that all beings will write, keep, meditate, divulge this Dharmaparyaya, by no other's power but the Lord's.

LS Chapter 13

4.109 ते च विशिष्टचारित्रप्रमुखा अप्रमेया असंख्येया बोधिसत्त्वा महासत्त्वा एतदूचुः तथा भगवन् करिष्यामो यथा तथागत आज्ञापयति। सर्वेषां च तथागतानां आज्ञां करिष्यामः परिपूरयिष्यामः। अल्पोत्सुको भगवान् भवतु यथासुखविहारी। द्वैतीयकमपि त्रैतीयकमपि स सर्वावान् बोधिसत्त्वगण एकस्वरनिर्घोषेण एवं भाषते स्म अल्पोत्सुको भगवान् भवतु यथासुखविहारी। तथा भगवन् करिष्यामो यथा तथागत आज्ञापयति। सर्वेषां च तथागतानां आज्ञां परिपूरयिष्यामः ।।

LS Chapter 22

te ca visistacaritrapramukha aprameya asamkhyeya bodhisattva mahasattva etaducuh tatha bhagavan karisyamo yatha tathagata ajnapayati sarvesam ca tathagatanam ajnam karisyamah paripurayisyamah alpotsuko bhagavan bhavatu yathasukhavihari dvaitiyakamapi traitiyakamapi sa sarvavan bodhisattvagana ekasvaranirghosena evam bhasate sma alpotsuko bhagavan bhavatu yathasukhavihari tatha bhagavan karisyamo yatha tathagata ajnapayati sarvesam ca tathagatanam ajnam paripurayisyamah

—*LS Chapter* 22

Simple meaning—The large number of Bodhisattvas headed by Visistacaritra spoke in one voice to the Lord Sakyamuni : We dedicate ourselves to do what the Tathagata commands; we shall fulfill the command of all Tathagatas. May the Lord be at ease as to what will happen after his departure. A second time, a third time, the entire host of Bodhisattvas spoke in one voice the same words : We shall do what the Tathagata commands; we shall fulfill the command of all Tathagatas. May the Lord be at ease as to what will happen after his departure. LS Chapter 22

4.110 एवमुक्ते गद्गदस्वरो बोधिसत्त्वो महासत्त्वस्तं भगवन्तं कमलदलविमलनक्षत्रराजसंकुसुमिताभिज्ञं तथागतं अर्हन्तं सम्यक्सम्बुद्धं एतदवोचत् तथाहं भगवन् करिष्ये यथा तथागत आज्ञापयति। गमिष्याम्यहं भगवन् तां सहां लोकधातुं तथागताधिष्ठानेन तथागतबलाधानेन तथागतविक्रीडितेन तथागतव्यूहेन तथागताभ्युद्गतज्ञानेन ।। LS Chapter 24

evamukte gadgadasvaro bodhisattvo mahasattvastam bhagavantam kamaladalavimalanaksatraraja--samkusumitabhijnam tathagatam arhantam samyaksambuddham etadavocat tathaham bhagavan karisye yatha tathagata ajnapayati gamisyamyaham bhagavan tam saham lokadhatum tathagatadhisthanena tathagatabaladhanena tathagatavikriditena tathagatavyuhena tathagatabhyudgatajnanena

—*LS Chapter* 24

Simple meaning—Thus addressed, the Bodhisattva Mahasattva Gadgadasvara said to the Lord Kamaladalavimalanaksatrarajasamkusumitabhijna: I dedicate myself to do as the Lord commands. I shall go to that saha-world by virtue of the Lord's resolution, by virtue of the Lord's power, by virtue of the Lord's might, by virtue of the Lord's decision, by virtue of the Lord's foresight. LS Chapter 24

Meditation and dedication : Selections from Bodhicaryavatara.

4.111 तस्माद् आवरणं हन्तुं समाधानं करोम्यहम्।
विमार्गात् चित्तमाकर्ष्य स्वावलम्बननिरंतरम् ।। BCA 8.186
तस्मान्मयानपेक्षेण कायस्त्यक्तो जगद्धिते।
अतोऽयं बहुदोषोऽपि धार्यते कर्मभाण्डवत् ।। BCA 8.184

tasmad avaranam hantum samadhanam karomyaham
vimargat cittamakarsya svavalambananirantaram
—BCA 8.186

tasmanmayanapeksena kayastyakto jagaddhite
ato'yam bahudoso'pi dharyate karmabhandavat
—BCA 8.184

Simple meaning—To destroy hindrance in the way of gaining knowledge, and to withdraw from the false path, I engage in meditation which provides complete rest to the mind.
BCA 8.186

Willingly I offer my services for the welfare of the world. Henceforth my body is borne, although it has many faults, like an instrument of karma in the service of all. BCA 8.184

4.112 आत्मानं चापरांश्चैव यः शीघ्रं त्रातुमिच्छति।
स चरेत् परमं गुह्यं परात्मपरिवर्तनम् ।। BCA 8.120
तस्माद्यथार्तिशोकाद् हि आत्मानं गोप्तुमिच्छसि।
रक्षाचित्तं दयाचित्तं जगत्यभ्यस्यतां तथा ।। BCA 8.117

atmanam caparamscaiva yah sighram tratumicchati
sa caret paramam guhyam paratmaparivartanam
—BCA 8.120

tasmadyathartisokad hi atmanam goptumicchasi
raksacittaam dayacittam jagatyabhyasyatam tatha
—BCA 8.117

Simple meaning—Whoever wants to quickly rescue himself as well as others, from suffering, should practice meditation which will enable the exchanging of one's self with the self of others. BCA 8.120)

As you wish to protect yourself from pain and suffering, you should practice that similar protection is available to everyone in the world. BCA 8.117

4.113 मयान्यद् दुःखं हन्तव्यं दुःखत्वादात्मदुःखवत् ।
अनुग्राह्या मयान्येऽपि सत्त्वत्वादात्मसत्त्ववत् ।। BCA 8.94
अतः परार्थं कृत्वापि न मदो न च विस्मयः ।
न विपाकफलाकांक्षा परार्थैकान्ततृष्णया ।। BCA 8.109

mayanyad duhkham hantavyam duhkhatvadatmaduhkhavat
anugrahya mayanye'pi sattvatvadatmasattvavat
—*BCA 8.94*

atah parartham kritvapi na mado na ca vismayah
na vipakaphalakamksa pararthaikantatrisnaya
—*BCA 8.109*

Simple meaning—Another person's sorrow is to be destroyed by me because it is sorrow like my own. All other persons are to be honored by me because their self is like my own. BCA 8.94

After having done something for the benefit of others, let there be neither arrogance nor desire for recognition, nor desire for any benefit in return. Let there be only thirst for the others' benefit. BCA 8.109

4.114 सुखभोगबुभुक्षितस्य वा
जनसार्थस्य भवाध्वचारिणः ।
सुखसत्रमिदं ह्युपस्थितम्
सकलाभ्यागतसत्त्वतर्पणम् ।। BCA 3.32
जगदद्य निमंत्रितं मया
सुगतत्वेन सुखेन चान्तरा ।। BCA 8.33

sukhabhogabubhuksitasya va
janasarthasya bhavadhvacarinah

sukhasatramidam hyupasthitam
sakalabhyagatasattvatarpanam —*BCA 3.32*
jagadadya nimantritam maya
sugatatvena sukhena cantara —*BCA 3.33*

Simple meaning—I recognize that all human beings should be able to carry on their lives, experiencing health and happiness. With the Buddha's blessings, such a joyful banquet can be prepared for the complete satisfaction of every being who participates in it. Today I dedicate my effort to bring about such a happy situation. BCA 3.32-33

4.115 काये नौबुद्धिमाधाय गत्यागमननिश्रयात्।
यथाकामं गमं कायं कुरु सत्त्वार्थसिद्धये ।। BCA 5.70
तथागताराधनमेतदेव
स्वार्थस्य संसाधनमेतदेव।
लोकस्य दुःखापहमेतदेव
तस्मान्ममास्तु व्रतमेतदेव ।। BCA 6.127

kaye naubuddhimadhaya gatyagamananisrayat
yathakamam gamam kayam kuru sattvarthasiddhaye
—*BCA 5.70*

tathagataradhanametadeva
svarthasya samsadhanametadeva
lokasya duhkhapahametadeva
tasmanmamastu vratametadeva —*BCA 6.127*

Simple meaning—After making the intellect, the driving force in the body, because it can come and go in a desired direction, make sure that the body moves in accordance with one's dedication for the sake of the well-being of people. BCA 5.70

For achieving the goal of "welfare of all", my immediate contribution is that I take a firm vow, viz. that I will try to destroy the sorrows of the world. I will view this as my worship of the Buddhas, and the source of my own happiness too. BCA 6.127

CHAPTER 5

Adaptation of the Message to Conditions in China

5.1 Our main interest in this chapter is to study how the social message of Mahayana Buddhism was adapted to conditions in China, from the first or second century onward. The Lotus Sutra was the main text of Mahayana at that time to convey this message. But the interest of the scholars who went to China, was not confined to the Lotus Sutra. Therefore they took with them other texts too. In fact, the journeys of the various scholars were not undertaken in any coordinated manner. And the two initial problems faced by all the scholars were : (i) how to translate the text from Sanskrit to Chinese, and (ii) how to obtain acceptance of local people who were already under the influence of Confucian and Daoist ideas.

Initial contacts and translations

5.2 During the first century, Buddhism had a strong presence within the Central Asian kingdoms that controlled most of the trade along the Silk Road which facilitated interaction between China and the outside world. So, when Emperor Ming of the Eastern Han dynasty in China had a dream about a golden deity, his advisers interpreted it in terms of the Buddha. The emperor sent a western-bound expedition that brought back to China two Buddhist scholars.

5.3 It is an interesting historical fact that a Buddhist scholar named Lokaksema went to China during the second century and translated the Pratyutpannasamadhi-Sutra into Chinese. The name of the scholar (Lokaksema) is meaningful and can be translated as "good of the world" (which happens to coincide with the social message of Mahayana). About Lokaksema's translation - capability, there is a comment by one of the historians that the language that he used was "broken Chinese".

5.4 The earliest extant Chinese translation of the Lotus Sutra was made by Dharmaraksa in the third century. However, the version which won the hearts of the Chinese people (and later, of others too) was prepared by the Buddhist scholar Kumarajiva in the beginning of the fifth century. Chinese historical records show that, for nearly two decades from 383, Kumarajiva was held as a captive by the Chinese army (for reasons not connected with religion). Such a long period of captivity was put to good use by Kumarajiva in the sense that he learned to speak and read Chinese. A change of military regime led to the release of Kumarajiva in the early years of the fifth century. Recognition of his extraordinary qualifications resulted in the appointment of Kumarajiva as the head of a large translation staff. Kumarajiva's version of the Lotus Sutra (prepared in 406) has proved to be so good that, in spite of the availability of so many more translations in the centuries that followed, it is often picked up as the first choice. Among other scholars who did the translation work of Buddhist texts, mention should be made of Hsuan-tsang (seventh century).

Adjustment with Confucian and Daoist organizations

5.5 Initially, Buddhism remained an elusive, foreign creed, practised primarily among the many Central Asian merchant communities that grew in Chinese trade centers. So it did not pose an institutional threat to the burgeoning Confucian orthodox tradition of statecraft or to the emergent Daoist religious groups. With the passage of time, it became clear to Buddhist missionaries that, while their interaction with

Daoists was rather smooth, they would need to make a good deal of adjustment in order to harmonize their relationship with the Confucian scholars.

5.6 The translators of Buddhist texts pointed out that they used the same Chinese character (jing she) for Buddhist vihara (monasteries), which denoted Daoist meditation chambers. The Han emperor Huan performed, during the second century, joint sacrifices to the deified Laozi and the Buddha. Many Daoists expressed an opinion that Laozi (who was reputed to have disappeared in the west after composing his "Daodejing") had become the Buddha. By the latter half of the fourth century, Daoist scriptural traditions originating in the south revealed the extent to which Buddhism had transformed the Chinese worldview. Daoist texts of that time show vague traces of Buddhist concepts, such as rebirth. Daoist texts of the fifth century represent an attempt to establish a harmonious synthesis with Buddhism, for example, an acceptance of the Buddhist ideas relating to "samsara". In terms of ritual practices, Daoists viewed Buddhism as the "religion of death" while they reserved for themselves the "religious functions of life".

5.7 Confucian scholars, who functioned as advisers to the Chinese emperor, criticized Buddhist monks, during the fifth century, for their lack of respect to governmental dignitaries. In fact, the critical attitude of Confucian scholars was directed, in general, against the world–renouncing practices of Buddhism. However, tables were turned by Empress Wuzhao in the seventh century. Her rise to power conflicted with traditional Confucian ideology that favored male rulers. She, therefore strengthened the Buddhist monasteries. But this, too, did not last long. The eighth century witnessed a strong anti-Buddhist policy by Emperor Wuzong.

5.8 From the tenth century onward, the Chinese society saw all-round progress in the form of expanding commerce, the spread of literacy, a flourishing printing and publishing industry, improved communication and transport systems. There was a rapid increase in the social and geographical mobility of the population. All of these factors facilitated the flow of religious ideas across regions, which helped the harmonization of the relationship between Confucianism and Daoism, on the one hand, and Buddhism, on the other. Harmonizing tendencies constituted a strong intellectual undercurrent among the elite, and struck even deeper roots in popular religion. New ideas relating to family and the local community did not require exclusive affiliation with any particular teaching. Instead, each was seen to have its role to play in the life cycles of families and communities, and thus the concepts and religious specialization associated with each could be drawn upon as needed. Because of these developments, Mahayana Buddhism became as much an integral part of the Chinese society, as Confucianism and Daoism. Such harmonization is reflected in the use of the expression "Three Teachings".

Role of Chinese scholars

5.9 Chinese scholars played a very important role in spreading the message of the Buddhist texts. A large number of commentaries on the Lotus Sutra were written, from time to time. Sadly, the earliest of these commentaries, viz. the one by Zhu Fachong (third century), has been lost. (Here we are referring to the work of Chinese scholars - not Dharmaraksa mentioned in para 5.4). Therefore, the great honor of writing the earliest, extant commentary on the Lotus Sutra is bestowed on Zhu Darsheng (360-434). From then on, almost eighty more commentaries on the Lotus Sutra have been written by Chinese scholars. Another important Mahayana text : "Awakening of Faith" is believed to be the original contribution of Chinese scholars. (See paras 5.23 and 5.25).

Three Sutras which people liked most

5.10 During the long history of Buddhism in China, the most popular religious movement was "Pure Land Buddhism".

This movement is characterized by devotion, a wish to be reborn in the Pure Land of Amitabha, and saved by the grace of the bodhisattva. The following three Sutras form the basis of this movement:-

(i) The Larger Sukhavativyuha Sutra
(ii) The Smaller Sukhavativyuha Sutra
(iii) Amitayurdhyana Sutra

5.11 Max Muller himself translated the two Sukhavati - Sutras, from Sanskrit to English, while Takakasu translated the Amitayurdhyana Sutra from Chinese to English—and the three were published in the same volume in 1894. Because of the great popularity of these three Sutras in China, we reproduce a summary, as given by Max Muller.

Summary of the Larger Sukhavativyuha Sutra

5.12 The Sutra begins with a dialogue between the Buddha and his famous disciple Ananda. Ananda observes that Buddha is in a state of spiritual exaltation and asks him what he is seeing or thinking. Thereupon Buddha relates how there was a line of eighty-one Tathagatas or Buddhas beginning with Dipankara and ending with Lokesvararaja. During the period of this Tathagata Lokesvararaja, a Bhiksu or Buddhist mendicant of the name of Dharmakara formed the intention of becoming a Buddha. He therefore went to the Tathagata Lokesvararaja, praised him in several verses, and then asked him to become his teacher and to describe to him what a Buddha and a Buddha country ought to be. After having received instruction, Dharmakara comprehended all the best qualities of all the Buddha countries, and prayed that they should all be concentrated in his own country when he himself becomes a Buddha. After long meditations, Dharmakara returns to Buddha Lokesvararaja and tells him in a long prayer what he wishes and wills his own Buddha country to be. This prayer forms the nucleus of the Sukhavativyuha ; it is, in fact, in the form of a prayer, a kind of prophecy of what, according to

Dharmakara's ideas, Sukhavati or the Land of Bliss ought to be. Dharmakara then became a Bodhisattva, a candidate for Buddhahood, and lastly a real Buddha. All this is related by Buddha Sakyamuni to Ananda, as a kind of vision of what happened ten kalpas ago. When Ananda asks Sakyamuni what has become of this Boddhisattva Dharmakara, Buddha answers that this original mendicant is now reigning in Sukhavati as the Buddha Amitabha. He then proceeds to describe Sukhavati where Amitabha dwells, and his description of Amitabha's country is very much the fulfilment of all that Dharmakara prayed for. Once Ananda is reproved by Buddha for not implicitly believing all he says about the marvels of Sukhavati, but afterwards the praises of Sukhavati and of its inhabitants are continued till nearly the end. In some verses recited by Buddha Sakyamuni, Amitabha himself, when questioned by the Buddha-son Avalokitesvara, explains that Sukhavati is what it is, in fulfilment of his prayers, when he was as yet living on earth. At last Ananda expresses a wish to see Amitabha, whereupon the Buddha sends a ray of light from the palm of his hand so that the whole world was inundated by its light, and not only Ananda, but every living being could see Amitabha and his retinue of Bodhisattvas in the Land of Bliss, while they in Sukhavati could see Sakyamuni and the whole world. Then begins the conversation between Sakyamuni and Ajita (instead of Ananda). Buddha explains to him how some of the blessed spirits in Sukhavati sit cross-legged in lotus-flowers, while others dwell shut up in the calyx of these flowers, the former being the firm believers in Amitabha, the latter being those who have entertained some doubt, and who have therefore to wait for five hundred years inside the calyx before they become full-blown, being debarred during all that time from seeing and hearing the Buddha. In conclusion, Buddha Sakyamuni exhorts Ajita to teach this treatise, the Sukhavati-vyuha, to all beings, and promises great rewards to all who will learn it, copy it, teach and explain it.

Summary of the Smaller Sukhavativyuha Sutra

5.13 The Smaller Sukhavativyuha lays great stress on the fact that people can be saved or can be born in the Land of Bliss, if only they remember and repeat the name of Buddha Amitabha, two, three, four, five, six or more nights before their death, and it distinctly denies that people are born in the Paradise of Amitabha as a reward or necessary result of good works performed in the present life. This would seem to take away one of the fundamental doctrines of Buddhism, namely the doctrine of karma, or of the continuous working of our deeds whether good or bad. Instead of the old doctrine, a new and easier way of salvation is here preached, viz. "As a man prayeth, so he shall be saved". It is what is known to us as salvation by faith rather than by works. The Larger Sukhavativyuha lays likewise great stress on prayer and faith in Amitabha, but it never neglects 'the stock of merit' as essential for salvation. It would almost seem as if this popular and easy doctrine had secured to itself the name of Mahayana, as meaning the Broad Way, in opposition to the Narrow Way, the Hinayana.

Summary of Amitayurdhyana Sutra

5.14 Vaidehi, consort of king Bimbisara of Magadha, seeing the wicked actions of her son Ajatasatru, began to feel weary of this world (called "Saha" which means the patient, much-enduring earth). Sakyamuni then taught her how to be born in the Pure Land Sukhavati, instructing her in the method of being born in that world, enumerating three kinds of good actions. The first is worldly goodness, which includes good actions in general, such as filial piety, respect for elders, loyalty, faithfulness, etc. The second is the goodness of "sila" or morality, in which there are differences between the priesthood and the laity. In short, however, all who do not oppose the general rule of reproving wickedness and exhorting to the practice of virtue are included in this goodness. The third is the goodness of practice, which includes that of the four Satyas or truths, and the six Paramitas or perfections. Besides these, all other pure and good actions, such as the reading and recital of the Mahayana Sutras, persuading others to hear the Dharma, and thirteen kinds of goodness to be practised by fixed thought, are comprised in this. Towards the end of the Sutra, Buddha says: 'Let not one's voice cease, but ten times complete the thought, and repeat the words: "Namo Amitabhaya Buddhaya", that is, "Adoration to Amitabha Buddha". This practice is the most excellent of all.' It is believed that the Chinese translation of this Sutra was done by Kalayasas in 424.

Max Muller's comment on the three sutras

5.15 The doctrine of Amitabha and his paradise Sukhavati acquired great popularity in China. We need not wonder when we see how easy salvation was made by it, particularly according to the teaching of the Smaller Sukhavativyuha and the Amitayurdhyana Sutra.

Brief history of Pure Land Buddhism

5.16 One of the most important figures in the early history of Pure Land Buddhism in China was Hui-yuan (334-416). He is usually associated with the founding of a Pure Land Society in 402. This group met regularly to meditate and to utter the vow to be reborn in the Western Paradise (presided over by Amitabha). Hui-yuan and his companions never went out into society to preach the Pure Land doctrine, because they were mainly hermits and retired scholars whose main purpose was to escape from the world. Yet Hui-yuan is often regarded as the first patriarch of the Pure Land School in China, mainly because he and his group served as an inspiration and model for later adherents.

Tan-luan

5.17 After Hui-yuan, the next important figure in the Pure Land movement was Tan-luan (476-542) whose home was in the north. For over a century, north China had become infiltrated with non-Chinese peoples and the cultural level in that area had declined. Inhabitants of that area were more inclined to a brand of Buddhism that emphasized magic, omens, mystic formulas, and prophecies, and a few Buddhist Sutras were even fabricated in that area to satisfy this tendency of the people. It was amidst such surroundings that Tan-luan was born.

5.18 On one occasion, Tan-luan recovered from a serious illness when he saw, in a dream, a heavenly gate open before him. This incident inspired him to search for an elixir that could bring about everlasting life. Initially, he became a disciple of a Daoist master. Subsequently, he met the Buddhist monk Bodhiruci who told him that Buddhism had a formula that was superior to that of the Daoist. After hearing about the Pure Land school, Tan-luan discarded the Daoist text and concentrated on the attainment of the Western Paradise.

5.19 Tan-luan's place in Buddhist history is based mainly on his efforts to spread the Pure Land teachings and practices among the whole of society. The oral invocation of the name "Amitabha" was popularised by him. As he neared death, his disciples, who numbered about three hundred, gathered around him to chant "Amitabha". In fact, Tan-luan is sometimes called the first patriarch of the Pure Land school. (Reference para 5.16—so there in no unanimity among historians as to which one of the two—Hui-yuan or Tan-luan—was the first patriarch).

Tao-cho

5.20 The next important leader of the Pure Land school was Tao-cho (562-645) who wrote "Collection of Essays on the Western Paradise". He argued that, during the period of decay, chanting the name of the Buddha was the most appropriate method of eradicating sins and ensuring rebirth in the Western Paradise. Tao-cho defended the Pure Land school from criticism leveled against it, especially by the Chan school.

Shan-tao

5.21 The next important leader of the Pure Land school was Shan-tao (613-681) who wrote "Commentary to the Sutra on Concentration". He became an innovative figure in Pure Land Buddhism by preaching that, side by side with the chanting of Buddha's name, meditation and worship should also be practiced. This opened up the possibility of reconciliation between Pure Land and Chan—a process that was completed later by Tzu-min.

Tzu-min

5.22 The task of popularizing as well as reforming the Pure Land school was practically completed by Tzu-min (680-748). He maintained that the tripod on which Buddhism rested—chanting, meditation, moral conduct—must all be followed with equal force, and none of the three was to be neglected.

Two Sutras that inspired the Chan school

5.23 The Chan school is important because it developed into Zen Buddhism (first in Japan and later in the west). The underlying idea of Chan is to adopt an open-minded approach as the means to enlightenment. The beginning of this school is traced back to the sixth century, the main sources of inspiration being the following two sutras:-

(i) Lankavatara Sutra

(ii) Mahayanasraddhotpada Sutra (or Treatise on the Awakening of Faith in Mahayana)

Summary of Lankavatara Sutra

5.24 The Lankavatara Sutra was probably composed during the fourth century. It contains a philosophical discussion on consciousness, reality, and mind-only. The main topic of discussion is the non-difference of identity between samsara (or the cycle of rebirth) and nirvana. As may as fifteen Chinese scholars have written commentaries on it (based on three Chinese translations).

Summary of Awekening of Faith

5.25 This text is probably of Chinese origin, written during the sixth century. An attempt is made, in this text, to adapt the doctrine of Buddha-nature (tathagatagarbha) to the Chinese way of thinking. It speaks of the Mahayana ideal of universal salvation and affirms the sanctity of life in this world. Its assumption of the inherent purity and enlightenment in the minds of all sentient beings provides a basis for the Chan school's doctrine of seeing one's nature and attaining Buddhahood.

Brief history of Chan school in China

5.26 Although Chan was introduced into China by an Indian monk, Bodhidharma, it was essentially a product of Chinese scholars. Chan rejected book learning as the basis of enlightenment, set aside all notions and theories of suffering and salvation, and relied upon day-to-day events, simple thinking and ordinary living as the means to enlightenment. It viewed enlightenment as descending upon one as a sudden shift in awareness, not because of elaborate study of the sutras and philosophies, nor worship of the images of the Buddha, but from a sudden opening of the mind. The Chan school discouraged the intellectual kind of pursuit of religion as it believed that a scholarly approach would tend to stiffen the mind and prevent it from experiencing the sudden flowering of Chan. By denigrating scriptural knowledge, the Chan masters were not promoting illiteracy, but were preparing the enlightenment-seekers to free themselves from opinionated intellectuality and scholarly affectations to emerge into a world of notionless experiences.

5.27 The word "Chan" is derived from the Sanskrit word "dhyana" meaning concentrated meditation or contemplation. "Dhyana" was an essential aspect of Chan Buddhism aimed at developing inner stillness and accumulation of pure energy among the practitioners. What Chan encouraged was not so much the mechanical aspects of meditation but rather the development of an unfettered and detached mind, that would not cling to anything and would not rest anywhere. Such a mind would flow with the natural flow of life, gathering nothing and gaining nothing. The goal of Chan was to experience the Buddha–mind in the most mundane tasks and conversations of day-to-day life. In short, Chan made living a deeply religious act aimed at breaking the encrusted layers of thought.

5.28 The Indian monk Bodhidharma (who introduced Chan in the sixth century) was the first patriarch of Chan school. The second patriarch was Hui-Ko who, as a disciple of Bodhidharma for six years, is believed to have achieved enlightenment. During an exile forced by persecution of Buddhists by Emperor Wu, Hui-Ko met and trained Seng-tsan to become his successor and the third patriarch.

5.29 Nothing spectacular has been recorded about the fourth patriarch (Tao Hsin), and the fifth (Hongren), but the sixth patriarch (Huineng) is remembered as a legendary master. In the famous text "Platform Sutra of the Sixth Patriarch", Huineng is depicted as an illiterate and impoverished layman, whose grandfather had been banished to the far south, and who supported his mother by the very humble endeavour of collecting firewood. Hard working and filial, in spite of his total lack of social advantages, Huineng possessed innate spiritual insight. This gift led him to the monastic training center of Hongren, who soon recognized his (i.e. Huineng's) extraordinary qualifications. As the sixth patriarch of Chan, Huineng stressed the doctrine of "sudden" teaching, whereby enlightenment occurs in a single instantaneous transformation. This is contrasted with the doctrine of "gradual" teaching whereby one moves toward enlightenment through progressive stages.

5.30 Although two of the famous schools of Chan (or Zen) had their development (later) in Japan, their start took place in China. Specifically, Soto's linkage was with Tsao-tung, and Rinzai's linkage was with Lin-chi.

Tsao-tung

5.31 This Chinese Chan-sect takes its name from the two founders, Tsao-shan and Tung-shan, who in turn had taken their names from the mountains on which they had their base. Tsao-tung emphasized the "Chan of silent enlightenment" and stressed the importance of sitting in meditation (zazen). The meditation is centered on the fundamental unity of Absolute and Relative.

Lin-chi

5.32 The Lin-chi sect was founded by I-hsuan, but it rose to its highest point under Yang-chi. This sect made use of Koan, which are, so to speak, undeveloped themes that often illogically confound the intellect and appeal to the intuition for understanding. Of course, the Koan are not viewed as an end, but as "helpful means" to enlightenment. The use of "stick" was introduced in this sect by Te-shan.

Avatamsaka Sutra inspiring Huayan and Kegon schools

5.33 The Chinese version of Avatamsaka Sutra is called Huayan Jing and its popular name in English is Flower Garland Sutra. The Huayan school is one of the uniquely Chinese traditions of Buddhism, and it spread to Japan as Kegon school.

Summary of Avatamsaka Sutra

5.34 The Sanskrit text of Avatamsaka Sutra is partly lost but the Chinese translations (the first done by Buddhabhadra in the fifth century and the second done by Siksananda in the seventh century) have been preserved. "Mutual interpenetration of all phenomena" is one of the main topics of this Sutra, and it is explained by means of the images of Indra's net of jewels. In the heaven of the god Indra, there is a vast net that extends infinitely in all directions. Each knot of the net holds a gleaming jewel, and because the net is limitless in size, it contains an infinite number of jewels.

As the multifaceted surface of each jewel reflects all other jewels in the net, each of the reflected jewels also contains the reflections of all other jewels; thus there is an unending process of infinite reflections.

5.35 The Avatamsaka Sutra narrates the fascinating story of Sudhana who travels throughout India from one teacher to another, in an attempt to learn about the cultivation of the bodhisattva path, with its distinct stages, practices and realizations. The Sutra depicts the bodhisattva path in terms of fifty-two stages, which include ten faiths, ten abodes, ten practices, and ten dedications. Sudhana's teachers explain to him all these stages, one by one.

Brief History of Huayan school

5.36 The Huayan school is especially known for its comprehensive and rarefied system of religious philosophy, which is widely regarded as a pinnacle of doctrinal development in medieval Chinese Buddhism. While the Huayan patriarchs incorporate the main streams of Mahayana scholasticism originating in India, they also reveal an unmistakably Chinese concern for harmony and balance.

5.37 The first patriarch of Huayan school, Dushun (also known as Fashun) was a famous meditation master of the seventh century. His historical position in the doctrinal evolution of Huayan is based on his reputed authorship of Fajie guanmen (Discernments of the Realm of Reality). This is a seminal text that formulates some of the basic principles and themes of the mature Huayan system, most notably the causal relationship between principle (li) and phenomena (shi).

5.38 The second patriarch of Huayan school, known as Zhiyan, wrote a long commentary on Huayan Jing, the primary scripture of the school. In it, he formulated some of the key doctrines that became hallmarks of Huayan thought, such as nature origination (xingqi) and conditioned origination of the realm of reality (fajie yuanqi).

5.39 The third patriarch of Huayan school, known as Fazang, was a prolific writer. He was closely associated with Siksananda's translation of Huayan Jing, undertaken under imperial auspices. Fazang's illustrious career was greatly helped by the unflagging patronage of Empress Wu. A record of Fazang's teaching presented to the Empress is preserved as "Treatise on the Golden Lion". The Empress was so impressed by Fazang's teaching that she bestowed on him the honorific name"Xianshou". Because of that, the Huayan school is also often called the "Xianshou School". Fazang's writings include an authoritative commentary on "The Awakening of Faith".

5.40 The fourth patriarch of Huayan school, known as Chengguan, earned great reputation because he was a scholar of Confucian and Daoist classics also. During his long monastic career (he died at the age of 101), he served under seven emperors. The imperial honors bestowed on him included the titles of national teacher, grand recorder of monks, and controller of the clergy. He is known for his monumental commentary on Siksananda's translation of the Huayan Jing. He was also the first Huayan scholar to incorporate some of the ideas of the Chan school into the texts of his own school.

5.41 The fifth and the last patriarch of Huayan school, known as Zongmi, continued the task of harmonizing the doctrines of the two schools (Chan and Huayan). He authored a number of works that cover a wide range of topics. He also introduced changes in his doctrinal taxonomy by including the teachings of Confucianism and Daoism.

5.42 Beyond China, the Huayan doctrine entered Korea and Japan (where it was known as Kegon). Huayan religious philosophy still retains its relevance to vital human concerns and has stimulated a significant cross–fertilization of ideas and viewpoints with modern philosophical and humanistic movements, including Engaged Buddhism and environmentalism.

Lotus Sutra inspiring Tientai school

5.43 The founder of the Tientai school (in the sixth century), known as Chih-i (or Zhiyi), was inspired by the Lotus Sutra in such a special way that he sang praises of this Sutra in a unique manner. He is believed to have attempted to make sense of the many Buddhist texts, contradictions between texts, and their doctrinal differences translated into Chinese. He thus created a five-fold historical outline : the Avatamsaka period witnessed the Buddha teach after his enlightenment in a state of ecstatic beatitude that lasted only three weeks because people could not understand the Buddha's message; the Agama period lasted twelve years with the Buddha teaching the Four Noble Truths and dependent origination, but he did not teach the full truth; the Vaipulya period lasted eight years, during which the Buddha did not teach the full truths of Mahayana, but he did teach about the superiority of the bodhisattva; a period lasting twenty-two years involved teaching about the Prajnaparamita and its doctrine of emptiness; and finally the Lotus Sutra that occurred during the final eight years of the Buddha's life, at which time he taught about the absolute identity of opposites and that all paths unite in a single vehicle (ekayana).

5.44 The name of the Tientai school is derived from the mountain (Mount Tientai) which was the site of the head temple of the school (and part-time residence of Zhiyi). Recent researchers have revealed that Zhiyi's doctrinal writings were consolidated, in the eighth century, by Zhanran, who interacted with other schools too, particularly Huayan and Chan.

Vimalakirti-nirdesa Sutra, a favorite of laymen

5.45 The Sanskrit text of this Sutra is lost but several Chinese translations are available (including one prepared by Kumarajiva in the fifth century). A layman, Vimala, embodying the ideal of the bodhisattva, is the principal character of this Sutra.

Summary of the Vimalakirti-nirdesa Sutra

5.46 Out of sympathy with the suffering of all beings, and as a strategy adapted to the circumstances, a layman, Vimala, feigns a serious illness. The Buddha instructs each of his sravaka and bodhisattva disciples to go and ask about his (i.e. Vimala's) health. All those addressed by the Buddha are reluctant to go, having been humiliated by Vimala's comparatively greater wisdom earlier. Only Manjusri agrees. All the others then go there to see what happens. Vimala asks each bodhisattva, in turn, how one enters non-dualism. Manjusri offers the ultimate insight that all dharmas are beyond discourse. The Sutra says that even Manjusri is trumped by Vimala, who remains silent when asked for his answer.

What appealed to the Chinese?

5.47 The portrayal of Vimala's wisdom had much to do with the popularity of this Sutra in China. Here was a layman, rich and powerful, a brilliant conversationalist, a respected householder who surrounded himself with the comforts of life, but who was also a faithful and wise disciple of the Buddha. The educated elite of the Chinese society must have felt that here was a model that they could emulate, for though Vimala was a Buddhist, he could very easily have been taken for a Confucian gentleman.

Modernization of Buddhism in the first half of 20th century

5.48 Tai-hsu or Taixu (1890-1947) was a Buddhist monk who launched a movement to modernize the religion and to revitalize it. His reforms called for a regeneration of the clergy, the rededication of Buddhist property for the benefit of the people, and the renewed study of the religious doctrines. In 1929, he organised a Chinese Buddhist Society. At the international level, he encouraged contacts with Buddhists of other countries, particularly Japan where reforms had already been made. Taixu is credited with coining the phrase " Buddhism for human life".

5.49 Another great leader was Hsu Yun (1840-1959). He is believed to have achieved enlightenment at age 55. Thereafter he worked as a bodhisattva, teaching precepts, explaining sutras, and restoring old temples. He travelled extensively and strengthened contacts with Buddhist scholars in different countries. He remained in China during World War II, and also after the establishment of the People's Republic of China, rather than escape to the safety of Hong Kong or Taiwan.

5.50 Still another great reformer was Yinshun (1906-2006), who was the primary successor of his teacher Tai-hsu (referred to in para 5.48). He reformulated and added academic sophistication to the content of his teacher's rallying rhetoric of "Buddhism for human life", and coined the new slogan "Humanistic Buddhism". His writings have been published as "Anthology of the Wondrous Clouds" and "Anthology of the Flower Rains". Taiwanese Buddhists have been inspired by Yinshun.

Status of Buddhism under the Communist regime

5.51 Soon after the communists came to power in China in 1949, Buddhists were forced to realize that the basic antagonism of Marxism toward religion could not be challenged. Step by step, opportunities for religious practice were reduced and ordination was restricted. Particularly at the time of the Cultural Revolution, Buddhist practice practically disappeared from China. A softening of attitude took place thereafter. Opinions may differ as to what sort of compromise has been established between the Buddhists on the one hand, and the regulatory apparatus of the government, on the other. We feel that, for purposes of this book, it is not necessary to go into details, as far as this point is concerned.

Chapter 6

Nurturing and Development of the Message towards Success in Japan

6.1 In the preceding chapter, we summarized the long process of adaptation experienced by Mahayana Buddhism in China. Chinese scholars deserve credit, not only for making Buddhism an integral part of life in their own country for so many centuries, but also for passing on the message to Japan and other countries. In this chapter we give a brief account of how the message was nurtured and developed by a long chain of Japanese scholars, finally achieving success in the latter half of the twentieth century.

6.2 As in the case of China, here too our approach will be selective. So the climax of the success story achieved by "Engaged Buddhism" in Japan, will be preceded by short descriptions of the following schools:-

(i) Kegon

(ii) Tendai

(iii) Pure Land (presided over by Amida)

(iv) Zen

(v) Nichiren

Kegon

6.3 Kegon is a Japanese term used to translate the Chinese name for the Hua-yen school. Kegon was a major school during the Nara perid (710-784) of Japanese history. Like its Chinese predecessor, the Japanese school was an adherent of the Avatamsaka Sutra (Flower Ornament Sutra); and it was originally brought to Japan by Shinji, a Korean monk. It gained popularity at court because of the preaching of Ryoben. The emperor Shumu Tenna was politically intrigued by the message of the Bodhisattva Vairocana being the center of the universe, from whom all phenomena emanated. In contrast to the emperor's political interest in the school, ordinary Japanse people were never interested in any great numbers. So the school never really thrived in Japan beyond a small dedicated group of monks or scholars. During the Heian period (794-1185), Kegon was practically assimilated into the more popular Tendai school.

Tendai

6.4 Tendai was a Japanese school founded by Saicho (767-822) who had earlier studied at the Tien-tai school in China. Like the Chinese school (Tien-tai), Tendai accepted the Lotus Sutra as its basic text. Nevertheless, the Japanese school (Tendai) became eclectic by combining its own doctrine, scripture and popular esoteric rituals, with elements from other schools, such as Zen and Pure Land. The school (Tendai) became very wealthy and powerful, and it tried to eliminate competition by using club-wielding and torch-carrying warrior monks to destroy competing temples or to eliminate other groups. Such activities harmed the school in the sense that it fell into decay and became corrupt. Ryogen (912-985) temporarily revived Tendai, but decline set in again after his death. Some of the former Tendai monks became associated with other schools. Tendai's center on Mount Hiei was destroyed by the warlord Oda Nobunaga in 1571, but it was restored after his assassination. Eventually, Tendai was eclipsed by other schools.

Pure Land (presided over by Amida)

6.5 Pure Land Buddhism found a foothold in Japan during the tenth century. Genshin is recognized as one of the first leaders of this sect. He believed that the mere repetition of the name of Amida (i.e. the practice of nembutsu) was sufficient for salvation in the form of rebirth in the Pure Land. In 985, Genshin published a treatise containing his views on salvation, which he called "Ojo yoshu : A Collection of Essentials concerning Rebirth in Amida's Western Paradise". This text was based on a commentary to the Amitayurdhyana Sutra by the Chinese monk Shan-tao (Reference para 5.21). Nearly two centuries later, Genshin's work inspired Honen, who is usually recognized as the real founder of Japanese Pure Land School.

Honen

6.6 Honen's parents felt that priesthood would be appropriate to him. He studied religion at Mount Hiei where he showed great promise. Ordained a priest, he retired to Kurodani on the outskirts of Kyoto. Renouncing the world, he devoted himself to prayer. He is said to have read the Buddhist Tripitaka five times, but that did not satisfy him. Most important for him was the peace of religious life, in contrast to the period of civil wars through which he had lived. Finally, he is said to have achieved Enlightenment upon reading Genshin's Ojo yoshu. What touched his heart was the message that salvation depended not on one's own strength but the strength of another, that is , on the intervention of the Savior Amida. In 1175, Honen began to teach what he had learned, and this year is usually accepted as traditional for the founding of the Jo do sect.

6.7 In 1198, Honen wrote "Collected Passages on the Original Vow and the Nembutsu". This text included not only Amida Sutra and Shan-tao's commentary thereon, but also Honen's own interpretation. Priests at Mount Hiei criticized Honen's work, but he wrote an open letter of a conciliatory nature and forbade the slandering of other Buddhas besides Amida.

6.8 The emperor Toba II was friendly to Honen, but in 1207, a serious misunderstanding arose over the behavior of some Pure Land priests, and Honen was exiled to Tusa and later to Sanuki, on the northeast of Shikoku. His exile lasted only ten months, but he was not allowed to return to the capital until 1211. In March 1212, he fell ill and died, in his eightieth year.

6.9 Although Honen believed earnestly in his own ideas of salvation and his own way of Amida worship, he was unassertive in preaching them against the opposition of the older, established sects. His quality of not giving offence to other scholars won him the admiration of common people. The popular name of Honen's sect was "Jodo shu".

Shinran

6.10 The next important leader of Pure Land School was Honen's disciple Shinran (also known as Zenshin or Shakku). Orphaned early, Shinran entered Mount Hiei at the age of nine. But Tendai teachings did not satisfy him. He visited Nara and then returned to Mount Hiei. He had a dream about studying with Honen—and this he began to do in 1201. In 1224, Shinran published his teachings: "Kyogyoshinso: Doctrine, Practice, Faith, and Realization". This became the basic text of "Jodo shinshu" or the "True Pure Land Sect". The main characteristic of this sect was that it abolished monasticism, and permitted the marriage of the priesthood.

Ippen

6.11 Another successor of Honen was Ippen who was originally a Tendai priest. He founded a sect called "Ji" meaning "Time". Insisting that his teaching was the right religion for that time, Ippen publicly distributed cards bearing the inscription "namu Amida butsu", which meant "Honor to the Buddha Amida". To him, all Shinto gods also were manifestations of Buddhas. In consequence, the nembutsu was directed to Shinto divinities as well as to Buddhas. Ippen's mysticism brought him close to Zen.

Zen

6.12 The schools of Zen that currently exist in Japan are: Soto, Rinzai, and Obaku. Of these, Soto is the largest and Obaku the smallest. But historically, the first Zen temple that was built by Eisai in 1191, belonged to the Rinzai school.

Eisai

6.13 Coming from a family of Shinto priests, Eisai spent his youth in Tendai Buddhism. In 1168, he undertook his first trip to China, where he visited the Chan centers on Tien-tai. He was highly impressed by what he saw and felt that in such discipline lay the salvation of Japanese Buddhism. On a second trip to China in 1187, he wanted to travel to India, but his journey beyond the Chinese borders was opposed by the Chinese authorities. So he utilized the time that he had, by studying at the Zen center of Tien-tungshan until 1191. Eisai received the " seal of Enlightenment" in the Rinzai sect, and after returning to Japan, he built the first Rinzai temple in 1191, marking the start of the new sect.

6.14 Eisai's interest in Zen teachings was opposed by Tendai scholars who, protesting that he placed Zen above Tendai, sought to have the new sect outlawed. But Eisai had the support of the authorities who not only protected his sect but also awarded him the direction of the Kenninji (Kyoto). Eisai linked Zen to the national welfare, and in his tract: "The Spread of Zen for the Protection of the Land", he argued for establishing Zen as a recognized sect. But Kenninji was not a purely Zen institution, so Eisai was obliged to maintain places also for Tendai and Shingon worship. With the help of the authorities, Eisai brought Zen to KamaKura, where he established a Zen monastery. Thus began the close relationship between Zen and the military establishment.

6.15 Hakuin (1685-1768) is recognized as the second great leader of the Rinzai Zen sect. He was the youngest of five childern in a family belonging to the Nichiren sect. At fifteen he studied at the Zen temple of his village, where he received the name of Ekaku. Subsequently, he spent many years wandering from place to place, finally establishing himself in the Myoshinji, where he received the name "Hakuin". Besides commenting on numerous Sutras, he was a painter and a poet, but most of all he was a tireless worker among the people. He organized and revivified Koan Zen. He was particularly devoted to making his kind of Buddhism understandable to common people.

Introduction of Soto Zen by Dogen

6.16 Dogen (1200-1253) belonged to an aristocratic family, and therefore received good education, specializing in Chinese poetry and classics. When Dogen was studying Tendai Buddhism on Mount Hiei, he became interested in the relation of Buddha-nature and Enlightenment. Subsequently, Dogen entered the Kenninji where Zen was mixed with Tendai and Shingon. He was not satisfied with the Rinzai type of Zen, so he departed for China, hoping to supplement his knowledge.

6.17 One of the things that struck Dogen profoundly was the stress which the Chinese Chan discipline laid upon daily work. Along with zazen and sutra reading, they considered daily work as an integral part of the religious life. At the Tien-tung monastery, Dogen participated in community life along with some five hundred persons. Despite his sincerity, however, Dogen did not win the "seal of Enlightenment" which he had sought. As a result, he set out on a life of wandering, acquainting himself with the various Chinese sects and other teachings. In 1225, Dogen became a disciple of Ju-ching, who was a severe master, making liberal use of the punishing stick. Finally, Dogen received the "seal of Enlightenment" and the cloak of patriarch in the Tsao-tung sect (Reference para 5.31).

6.18 In 1227, Dogen returned to Japan, without sutras, without pictures or images, and established himself in the

Kenninji. There he composed a short treatise on the practice of meditation, entitled: "General Teaching for Zazen". By 1230, he had moved onto the temple of Anyoin of Fukakusa, which fast became a Zen center, visited by many pilgrims from nearby Kyoto. Dogen taught the realizing of one's Buddha-nature by means of practice and discipline, through Zazen. His great work : "Shobogenzo: Treasury of Knowledge of the True Law" was a treatise on Zen practice and doctrines from the standpoint of his own Enlightenment. In 1233, Dogen was given a large building in the temple grounds of the Gokurakuji, and here he was joined by his most famous disciple, Ejo. In 1236, Dogen constructed a new temple, the Koshohormji, complete with Zen hall. This was the first purely Zen temple in Japan, and in it Dogen reached the climax of his career. Later, in 1245, he founded the famous "Temple of Enduring Peace", which became the principal training center of the Soto sect. Dogen was awarded the honorific title of Buppozenji in 1250.

6.19 Unlike Eisai, Dogen was uncompromising towards other sects, and unwilling to associate his Zen with them. His attitude earned him the hatred of the Tendai monks on Mount Hiei. As a result, in 1247, he was obliged to leave the capital for some time and go into exile. He finally visited Kyoto in 1253, where with his disciple Ejo, he went for medical care and where in the same year he died.

6.20 Dogen minimized the value of the koan and stressed that of zazen - a discipline of meditation without thought of acquisition or attainment. Dogen referred to the experience of Buddha himself and said that his (i.e. Buddha's) attaining Enlightenment under the Bodhi tree was the "proved" method. Based on this, Dogen opposed the Rinzai use of koan, which he viewed as too self-assertive a method, stressing the attainment of a given state and overemphasizing mental perception. In Dogen's opinion, the "whole man" should participate in the experience of Enlightenment.

6.21 Zen masters fostered the growth of the cult of tea. Dogen established a center of pottery production which turned out an improved quality of tea cup. The practice of drinking tea as well as of frequenting the tea hut, became a formalized ritual presided over by Zen ideas, and it was meant to provide a Zen experience. The drinking of the non-alcoholic beverage in surroundings bound up with nature provided the means of perceiving the divine in the common being. The outside of the tea hut, which is continually weathering, suggests that life is constant change. Various aspects of the garden stand for selflessness: the stepping-stones, willing to be trodden upon; the basin, whose water willingly takes away impurities; in a corner, a stone lantern, whose wick consumes itself so that there may be light. Within the tea hut itself is absolute peace. Rising incense charms by its odor but recalls also the aspiration that man should feel toward the celestial. The tea itself is served in simple, everyday containers which indicate that religious experience is after all an ordinary thing; just as clay is transformed into the tea cup, so man is transformed into a vessel capable of receiving Enlightenment and Buddhahood.

Obaku sect

6.22 Ingen (1592-1673) was a Chinese priest who introduced the Obaku sect in Japan, which has much in common with the Rinzai Zen. Both zazen and koan are considered the best approaches to satori (Enlightenment), but the nembutsu, or invocation of the name of Amida, is also esteemed. Amida is honored, not as a transcendental Buddha, but as Buddha-spirit in daily life. The Pure Land is viewed as lying in one's heart only. The Obaku sect received support from richer sections of the society.

Nichiren (1222-1282)

6.23 For purposes of this book, we attach special importance to Nichiren. He was born on 16 February 1222, in a fisherman's family of Kominato in the province of Awa. His original name was Zennichi-maru, but at eleven he was ordained under the religious name of Rencho. He was instructed in "nembutsu" of Pure Land Buddhism, but from the very beginning he had doubts about the efficacy of this invocation. This doubt led to his decision to unify and reform the Buddhism of his day. He spent ten years at Mount Hiei where he became convinced that the way the Tendai doctrine was practised at that time needed to be modified. His desire to return to a pure form of Tendai created difficulty for him and he was forced to leave Mount Hiei. In 1253, he returned to his former monastery at Kiyozami. There he preached his new doctrine, that the salvation of the degenerate age lay in the Lotus Sutra. Rather than calling on the name of a particular Buddha, say Amida, one should call on the eternal Buddha or the Buddhist law itself. He proclaimed a kind of nembutsu of his own creation; "Reverence to the wonderful Law of the Lotus". Subsequently, this invocation became the slogan of the Nichiren sect. Besides faith in the Lotus, Nichiren preached the importance of one's own efforts and of the Bodhisattva ideal of perseverance and sacrifice. The date of his first sermon (28 April) is observed as the date when the Nichiren school was founded. (The literal meaning of Nichiren is "Sun-lotus").

6.24 At his monastery in Iwamoto, Nichiren wrote his famous text: "Treatise on Establishing Right and the Peace of the Country", elaborating his belief in the close relation between religion and national welfare. Although the defacto existence of the close relation between religion and nation was routinely accepted at that time, Nichiren gave it the status of a basic principle.

6.25 Nichiren announced his own formulation concerning the Buddhist concept of "mappo" or " decline of dharma". He divided Buddhist history into three periods:

(i) shobo or initial period (Theravada)
(ii) zobo or middle period (Mahayana)
(iii mappo or end-period (beginning 1050 CE)

Nichiren firmly believed that only the belief in the Lotus Sutra could lead to salvation in the end-period.

6.26 Nichiren adopted an attitude of "intolerance" which characterized his writings as well as other activities. For example, he did not consider the killing of heretics as murder; indeed, in his opinion, it was the duty of the government to see that they are put to death. Nichiren was particularly critical of Honen's doctrine (Belief in the Pure Land of Amida).

6.27 Nichiren picked up, from the fifteenth and twenty-second chapters of the Lotus Sutra, the statement of the Bodhisattva Visistacaritra, that he had preached the Dharma after Sakyamuni's death and devoted himself to the spreading of Buddhism. Nichiren identified himself with this Bodhisattva, who had worked in this world in its age of degeneration, to bring salvation to all.

6.28 Similarly, Nichiren picked up, from the twentieth chapter of the Lotus Sutra, the eye-opening experience of the Bodhisattva Sadaparibhuta. Although this Bodhisattva addressed people as "Bodhisattva", believing that each person had the Buddha–nature within him (or her) and would ultimately be saved, still people insulted and reviled him. Nichiren derived consolation from this narration of the Lotus Sutra, because he himself had received insults in his life.

6.29 Elaborating his views on the "mappo" (reference para 6.25 above), Nichiren warned that Mongols would attack Japan (and this did happen). Probably, Chinese priests associated with him had got this advance information about Mongol hostility, and Nichiren conveyed the same to Japanese authorities. But Nichiren linked this with "mappo" and argued that the Mongol invasion would take place because of the false religious views held by the Japanese at that time. Nichiren believed that political and spiritual salvation lay in the rectification of such false views.

6.30 Nichiren's religious convictions were so strong that he attacked all other forms of Buddhism. He even attacked the government. As a consequence of such attacks, Nichiren had a sense of insecurity, and he left KamaKura. After some time, he came back, but his attacks on all others continued as before. In 1261, he was banished by the government to the peninsula of Isu.

6.31 Nichiren utilized the period of exile for making an intensive study of the Lotus Sutra. His inner voice told him that he was the divinely designated teacher of that age.

6.32 Nichiren was released from Isu in 1263. But there was still no change in his attitude towards those who held, according to him, false religious views. He bitterly criticized all other sects, concentrating his criticism on the Pure Land group. As a result of all these attacks, he was sentenced to death, the execution to be carried out on the island of Sado in 1271. At this point, it was nothing short of a miracle that Nichiren got a stay of execution—and his followers saw in this a divine intervention.

6.33 After getting a miraculous stay of execution, Nichiren spent three years on the island of Sado. He utilized this time for writing his famous book: "The Eye Opener". In this text, he set forth his three vows:-

(i) That he would be the pillar of Japan

(ii) That he would be the eyes of Japan

(iii) That he would be the great vessel of Japan, that is, the container of the religious truth that was to revivify the country.

6.34 In 1274, Nichiren was released and recalled to Kamakura, where he settled along with a few disciples. The final years of his life were spent in a continual struggle for the Union of Japan and for his sect, until in the end he retired to his hermitage at Ikegami. He died there on 13 October 1282, reciting stanzas from the Lotus Sutra.

6.35 Although Nichiren thought that his interpretation of the Lotus Sutra was perfect, it is obvious that he did not pay adequate attention to the basic Buddhist message of Ahimsa (non-violence). This inadequacy could have been averted if, along with the Lotus Sutra, Nichiren had studied Bodhicaryavatara. Apparently, this book of Shantideva (written in Sanskrit in the eighth century) was not translated, at that time, into Chinese/ Japanese. Non-observance of Ahimsa was the main factor causing problems for Nichiren. Subsequently, the same factor created serious problems for Nichiren's followers during the first half of the twentieth century.

Hard time for all Buddhists during 1895-1945

6.36 The fifty-year period, 1895-1945, proved to be very difficult for Japanese Buddhists. There were a series of wars, namely, Sino-Japanese War, Russo-Japanese War, War with China, and finally, World War II. During the wars, the Japanese Government did not tolerate any dissenting voice. In 1937, the Ministry of Education published "Cardinal Principles of the Nation" which made it obligatory for all Japanese people to sacrifice themselves, if need be, for the good of the nation. State Shinto was the ideology of the nation and the Buddhist organizations were given no choice but to support it.

6.37 In 1938, Takasa Nichiko, the administrative head of the Nichiren sect, supported by leading members of the clergy, formed "The Association for the Practice of Imperial-way Buddhism". This Association declared that the principal image of adoration at that time was not the Buddha, but His Majesty, the Emperor. Such declarations adversely affected the prestige which the Nichiren sect had enjoyed till then, not only in Japan but in other countries too.

Notable persons who tried to Strengthen Buddhism

6.38 Tanaka Chigaku (1861-1939) argued that the time for monks and nuns was over, and that Buddhist clergy in Japan should view themselves as lay bodhisattvas instead. He did not view married clergy as a degeneration of Buddhism into a family business, but rather an opportunity to keep the temples alive as centers of lay practice. He advocated that an academy should be set up for the wives of priests so that they could assume equal responsibility for the care of the temples. Tanaka was convinced that lay Buddhism was the way of the future. With this end in view, he founded "Nation's Pillar Society". He referred to his movement as Nichirenshugi (or Nichirenism) because he viewed it as a new and more appropriate way of practising Nichiren Buddhism. In many ways, Tanaka inspired later groups like the Reiyukai and Rissho Kosei Kai.

6.39 Seno Giro (1889-1961) was one of the few Nichiren Buddhists who tried to resist (unsuccessfully) the war-time restrictions. In 1931, he founded "The Youth League for Revitalizing Buddhism". The League was composed of social activists who were critical of capitalism, internationalistic in outlook, and committed to an intersectarian and more practical form of Buddhism that would work for social justice and world peace. Their motto was "Carry the Buddha on your backs and go out into the streets". They gathered signatures and worked to change laws to help poor farmers, and other marginalized people in Japanese society. They can be called the first "engaged Buddhists" in modern Japan.

6.40 Fuji Nichidatsu (1885-1985) was ordained in the Nichiren sect as the age of 19. At age 32, he began to beat the hand drum and chant Odaimoku as his basic practice in order to fulfill the teachings of his sect and bring peace through the establishment of Wonderful Dharma. To further his efforts, he founded the Nipponzan Myohoji while doing missionary work in China and Manchuria in 1917. In 1931, he travelled to India and met Mahatma Gandhi. After the devastation caused by World War II, particularly the atomic bombings of Hiroshima and Nagasaki, Fuji became determined to bring about world peace by marching all over the world, beating the drum and chanting Odaimoku, and also through the construction of peace pagodas all over the world, beginning with India and Japan. Even after the death of the founder in 1985, the organization (Nipponzan Myohoji) continued to implement the program started by Fuji.

Socially active organizations

6.41 Nipponzan Myohoji. This organization is known in the west for its Peace Pagodas in many locations around the world. It is also known for many high profile peace pilgrimages undertaken by its followers. One of the most prominent of these was the 1994-95 pilgrimage from Auschwitz to Hiroshima by way of Bosnia, Iraq, Cambodia and other countries then experiencing the effects of war. That pilgrimage was known as "The Interfaith Pilgrimage for Peace and Life".

6.42 Soka Gakkai. The starting date of this famous organization is usually taken to be 18 November 1930 when "Soka Kyoiku Gakkai" was founded by the Japanese educator Tsunesaburo Makiguchi and his colleague Josei Toda. Both these leaders had a hard time during World War II. For refusing to cooperate with the government, they were arrested in 1943. The first president of the organisation (Makiguchi) died in prison in 1944. Josei Toda was released from prison in July 1945, just weeks before the first use of the atomic bomb. He, as the second president, worked hard to rebuild the organization during the 1950's. On 3 May 1960, Daisaku Ikeda became the third president. During his presidency, which lasted till 23 April 1979, there was a big expansion and diversification in the activities of the organization. In 1975, Soka Gakkai International (SGI) was founded. On its website, SGI defines its purpose as follows:

For SGI members, Buddhism is a practical philosophy of individual empowerment and inner transformation that enables people to develop themselves and take responsibility for their lives. As lay believers and engaged Buddhists, SGI members strive in their everyday lives to develop the ability to live with confidence, to create value in any circumstances and to contribute to the well-being of friends, family and community. The promotion of peace, culture and education is central to SGI's activities.

6.43 Hiroshi Hojo was the fourth president of Soka Gakkai (from 24 April 1979 till 17 July 1981). The fifth president Einosuke Akiya had a long and eventful tenure (from 18 July 1981 till 8 November 2006). On 9 November 2006, the sixth president, Minoru Harada took charge of the organization's multi-dimensional activities. The contribution of this organisation at the international level is so well known that we do not consider it neccssary to write about it in this book.

6.44 Reiyukai and Rissho Kosei Kai. We mention these two organizations together, because Rissho Kosei Kai was founded by two leaders who were formerly with Reiyukai. To begin with, it was in 1920 that Kakutaro Kubo and Kimi Kotani founded Reiyukai as an Association of Spiritual Friends. This is a lay organization—meaning that there are no priests — associated with Nichiren Buddhism. Reiyukai considers itself the grandfather of lay-based new religions devoted to the Lotus Sutra and ancestor veneration.

6.45 Rissho Kosei Kai was founded on 5 march 1938 by Nikkyo Niwano and Myoko Naganuma, both former members of Reiyukai. The reason why they left Reiyukai was that, at a meeting attended by them, the president of Reiyukai made remarks that lectures and study of the Lotus Sutra were out of date. After hearing this and consulting with each other, they determined that they could not support such ideas.

6.46 The two main characteristics of Rissho Kosai Kai are;

(i) They consider themselves as a Buddhist organization in direct line of descent from Shakyamuni Buddha. The basis of the organization is the principle of peace and liberation discerned by Rev. Nikkyo Niwano.

(ii) They emphasize the practical application of Buddhist teachings. Members of the organization, with faith in the Buddha, apply his teachings in their daily lives. They recite the Lotus Sutra, mornings and evenings, strive to learn the teachings at local temples through counseling sessions and doctrinal lectures, as well as significant events and ceremonies, and guide other people to the faith by sharing the teachings and their experiences.

6.47 It was during the 1960's that Rissho Kosei Kai began to take active part in interfaith co-operation. Nikkyo Niwano had a private audience with Pope Paul VI at the Second Vatican Council in 1965. Subsequently, in 1969, he attended the 20th World Congress of International Association for Religious Freedom (IARF). In 1970, he helped to form the World Conference of Religions for Peace (WCRP), assuming leadership role therein on a continuing basis.

6.48 Rissho Kosei Kai has supported UNICEF since 1979. It has also supported and participated in a number of UN programs, including the second Special Session of the UN General Assembly devoted to Disarmament held in 1982.

6.49 In 1991, Nikkyo Niwano stepped down as President of Rissho Kosai Kai, and his son Nichiko Niwano assumed charge. In 1994, Nichiko's daughter, Mitsuyo Niwano, was made Vice President and designated successor. Five years later, in 1999, Nikkyo Niwano passed away.

6.50 In 2008, Rissho Kosei Kai International of North America was established due to growth of interest in the organization in USA and Canada. As of 2010, the organization has established centers in 20 countries.

CHAPTER 7

Challenges followed by Undaunted Work in Korea, Vietnam, and Taiwan

7.1 In this chapter, we shall review briefly how the social message of Mahayana Buddhism faced challenges in Korea, Vietnam, and Taiwan. Each of these countries presents a fascinating story of how the message not only survived the challenges but also moved ahead with renewed vigor.

Korea

7.2 Buddhism was officially introduced from China to Korea in the year 372. At that time, the Korean peninsula was divided into three kingdoms:

(i) Koguryo in the north

(ii) Paekche in the southwest

(iii) Silla in the southeast

Of the three, Koguryo was the first to welcome the Chinese monk-envoy, named Sundo, who brought with him Buddhist images and scriptures, from northern China. Next, it was Paekche where Buddhism was introduced by scholars from southern China. Finally, it was in the year 527 that Silla officially recognized Buddhism.

7.3 Buddhism brought into Korea a number of new religious practices and ideas. Buddhist monks were clearly set apart from the rest of the society. Images of Buddha and

Bodhisattvas offered a clear focus for worship and devotion. Buddhist scriptures contained not only moral teaching but also soaring philosophical ideas. In addition, a host of new cultural phenomena accompanied Buddhism, including architecture, craftsmanship, a writing system, and medicine. Although many years passed before the philosophical subtleties of Buddhism were fully appreciated, its material culture alone was sufficient to win the hearts of the Korean kings and nobles, as well as the common people.

7.4 Although the Korean aristocrats welcomed Buddhism mainly for its material benefits, such as the protection of the state and the welfare of the families, many (Korean) monks were happy to study the Chinese Buddhist texts. Almost all the major Mahayana texts, which had played an important role in the formative period of Chinese Buddhism, were introduced into Korea. Subsequently, Korean monks played an important role in the transmission of Buddhism to Japan.

7.5 Among Korean scholars of the seventh century, the contributions of two monks were particularly important, viz. Uisang, and Wonhyo. The former (Uisang) went to China to study the Huayan texts (reference paras 5.36—5.42). On his return to Korea, Uisang became the founder of the Korean Hwaom (Huayan) school, the most influential doctrinal school in Korean Buddhism. He prepared the "Chart of the One-vehicle Dharma-realm of Huayan", which sets forth the gist of Hwaom philosophy in the form of 210 Chinese characters arranged in a square diagram. Uisang has the honor of founding many famous monasteries too.

7.6 The latter scholar (Wonhyo) was a prolific writer who produced eighty-six texts, of which twenty-three are still extant, either completely or partially. By the time Wonhyo was so active, most of the important sutras had reached Korea, and people often got confused due to differences between one text and another. It was Wonhyo's genius to interpret the various texts in a way that would reveal their underlying unity of concept, without sacrificing the distinctive message of each text.

7.7 But Wonhyo was more than a scholar-monk. He tried to embody in his own life the ideal of a bodhisattva who works for the well-being of all.Transcending the distinction between the sacred and the secular, he married a widowed princess, visited villages and towns, and taught people with the help of songs and dances.

7.8 Beginning in the latter part of the eighth century, Korea experienced political turmoil due to conflicts within the ruling class and the rise of local warlords. During this period, the Son or Chan school of Buddhism was introduced from China into Korea. Numerous Son centers were established, mostly in provinces far away from the capital (Kyongju) and under the patronage of local warlords. In this way, the "Nine Mountian School of Son" was established. In course of time, a conflict arose between the new school and the older schools, bifurcating the Korean Sangha.

7.9 As a result of the long political turmoil, a new dynasty "Koryo" came to power in the tenth century. The founder of this dynasty, Wangkon, attributed his political success to the protective power of the Buddhas. He constructed numerous Buddhist monasteries with a view to curbing evil forces. The state established a monks' examination system that was modelled on the civil service examination. Titles were conferred on the monks who passed the examination. In this way, the Buddhist Sangha became a part and parcel of the state bureaucracy, and the idea of "state-protection Buddhism" became firmly entrenched during the Koryo dynasty.

7.10 In the latter half of the eleventh century, a new school connected with the Tientai school of China (reference paras 5.43-44) was established in Korea. Prince Uichon (who became a monk) was responsible for this development. Uichon wanted his new school to balance doctrinal study and meditation.

7.11 In the twelfth century, a Son monk named Chinul led a quiet, monastic reform movement in order to purify the Koryo Sangha. After intensive study and research, Chinul established a comprehensive approach to Son that balanced "sudden enlightenment" with "gradual enlightenment". In this way he permitted both a Hwaom method of "sudden enlightenment" and the "extraordinary" method of Koan meditation. Chinul's approach became the foundation for the thought and practice of Korean Son Buddhism, from the twelfth century onward.

7.12 With the collapse of the Koryo regime in 1392, Buddhism started facing difficulties. The new dynasty "Choson" (1392-1910), which was built upon neo-Confucian ideology, severed its official relationship with Buddhism. Land holdings were confiscated and hundreds of monasteries were disbanded. Monks were not allowed to enter the capital city, the monks' examination system was abolished, and the various Buddhist denominations were forced to consolidate. Only two denominations, "Sonjong" and "Kyojong", were left, all others being absorbed into them.

7.13 It was during this period of persecution that the denominational identities of traditional Buddhist schools disappeared, and the ascendancy of "Son" began. Less dependent, perhaps, upon institutional and doctrinal structures, "Son" withstood the persecution better than "Kyo", and managed to maintain its tradition, deep in the mountain areas.

7.14 Buddhism experienced a short revival during the sixteenth century, thanks to Hyojong. Although a "Son" master, Hyojong demonstrated an accommodating attitude toward doctrinal studies. He argued that "Kyo" is the word of the Buddha, whereas "Son" is his mind. Although he believed in their essential unity, Hyojong taught that a monk's training should begin with "Kyo", but eventually the trainee must move on to "Son" in order to attain perfection.

Hyojong thus established the principle of "relinquishing Kyo and entering into Son", which is still followed among Korean monks.

7.15 Hyojong and his followers, especially Yujong and Yonggwan, played an important role in mobilizing the monks' militia against Japanese forces during the Hideyoshi invasion (1592-1599). Although Buddhist monks were held in contempt in the strongly anti-Buddhist Confucian society, they were ironically the salvation of the state during this national crisis. Many monks were subsequently given high honorific military titles, and their improved status continued for a while after the war.

7.16 On the whole, during the Choson period (till 1910), Buddhism remained largely confined to the countryside, isolated from mainstream intellectual and cultural life. Nevertheless, monks of high learning and character continued to flow into the Sangha, providing leadership during a difficult period.

7.17 During the Japanese colonization of Korea (1910-1945), Korean Buddhism faced new challenges. The Japanese policy towards Buddhism was inconsistent. Although the Japanese government lifted the ban on monks' entry into metropolitan areas and allowed most religious activities, the officials tried to control the Korean Sangha and to force its merger with one or another Japanese sect of Buddhism. The Monastery Act placed the Korean Sangha under political surveillance by imposing a hierarchical organisation on the monasteries and by requiring state approval for the appointment of the abbots. An important development in Korean Buddhism under colonial rule was the emergence of married priests, an influence of Japanese Buddhism, which eventually became a major source of conflict in the Sangha after 1945.

7.18 After 1945, a struggle broke out between celibate monks and married clergy over control of the monasteries, resulting in the schism of the Sangha in 1962 into two denominations: the celibate Chogye order, and the much smaller Taego order for married priests.Today, the Chogye order represents virtually all of Korean Buddhism.

7.19 In the early years of the twenty-first century, it is estimated that more than ten million Buddhists live in Korea, mainly in the South. Although some Buddhist monasteries exist in North Korea, the number of practising Buddhists is negligible. Many urban centers of Buddhism have been established in South Korea, drawing large numbers of middle-and upper-class citizens. Many monks with keen social conscience are leading movements dedicated to various social, political, and environmental causes, including the reconciliation of North and South Korea.

Korean scholars in the West

7.20 Seung Sahn was temple abbot in Seoul, but in 1972, he moved to USA. On the flight to Los Angeles, a Korean American passenger offered him a job at a laundry in Providence, Rhode Island. Seung Sahn founded the Providence Zen Center, which later became headquarters of Kwan Um School of Zen. Currently, the Kwan Um School has more than 100 Zen centers on six continents.

7.21 Another Korean Zen teacher, Samu Sunim, founded Toronto's Zen Buddhist Temple in the 1970's. He later became Head of the Buddhist Society for Compassionate Wisdom, which has temples in Ann Arbor, Chicago, and Mexico City.

7.22 Still another Korean scholar of international fame, is Pohwa Sunim who is head monk of the Hwagaesa International Zen Center, in Seoul. He founded several Zen centers in USA, including the Potomac Zen Center in Alexandria, Virginia, and the Baltimore Zen Center in Maryland.

Vietnam

7.23 There is evidence to believe that Buddhism reached Vietnam during the second century. At that time, Vietnam was a Chinese protectorate, known as Jiaozhou. During the next four centuries, Buddhist monks from China as well as India paid occasional visits to Jiaozhou. Similarly, Vietnamese scholars too went on pilgrimage to India as well as China, to visit Buddhist sacred places and to study the dharma. Some of the Vietnamese monks were well versed in Sanskrit and they assisted Indian and Chinese monks in translation work.

7.24 Vietnam gained independence from Chinese political hegemony in the tenth century. The early Vietnamese dynasties found in the Buddhist clergy a cultural force that could assist them with their political agenda. The founder of the Dinh dynasty (968-980) instituted a system of hierarchical ranks for court officials, Buddhist monks, and Daoist priests. The Ly dynasty (1010-1225) continued to draw support from Buddhism, and in return, they patronized Buddhism on a large scale. The Ly Kings also sent envoys to China to bring back Buddhist texts so that copies could be made and placed in the major monasteries. Some Chan classics thus found their way to Vietnam.

7.25 Under the Tran dynasty (1225-1400), Chan learning became more established with the arrival of Chinese Chan monks and Chan-related literature. The first Vietnamese Chan Buddhist school was founded around the year 1300. The most important accomplishment for Buddhism around the mid-fourteenth century was the composition, by Vietnamese scholars, of the text: "Outstanding Figures of the Chan Community".

7.26 But Buddhist fortunes suffered a setback from the fifteenth century onward. The advent of the (second) Ly dynasty (1428-1802) marked a resurgence of Confucianism. The Ly Kings passed restrictive measures against Buddhism. Still they allowed the establishment of Thien Buddhist schools.

7.27 The Nguyen dynasty (1802-1882) continued to favor Confucianism, which they considered to be a useful force in their efforts to centralise power. There was an attempt to depoliticize Buddhism because it was viewed as detrimental to the Confucian hierarchy. Although the majority of court officials were Confucian, Buddhism still appealed to aristocratic women and was favored by the masses. On the whole, the Nguyen era proved to be a period of ardent Buddhist scholarly activity.

7.28 Vietnam was under French rule from 1883 to 1945, and this presented new pressures for the Buddhists. Under foreign rule, Vietnamese Buddhists felt the need to create a more socially and politically engaged organization. Many eminent monks were patriots and leaders of insurgent movements. They were inspired by reform movements in other Asian countries, and in particular, by the Chinese monk Taixu (reference para 5.48). Buddhist magazines and periodicals in colloquial Vietnamese began to appear with a view to addressing political and social issues. During the 1930's, three new associations of Buddhist scholars were established in the three parts of Vietnam. All of them were guided and supported by learned clergy and lay people with exposure to western culture. There were attempts at consolidating the three associations into a unified sangha, but these efforts were hindered by the repressive policy of the French.

7.29 The end of the French colonial era did not bring any relief to Buddhists. Emperor Bao Dai of South Vietnam signed Decree No. 10, which followed the French policy of relegating all religions to the status of "public associations", with the exception of Catholic and Protestant missions. In 1955, the new head of South Vietnam, Ngo Dinh Diem, retained Decree No. 10. In 1957, Diem also eliminated the Buddha's birthday (Vesak) from the list of official holidays. However, Diem's discriminatory policy against Buddhism led to strong resistance movements during the 1960's, which ultimately resulted in the overthrow of his government.

7.30 A controversial feature of the Buddhist resistance was the practice of "self-immolation". Vietnamese monks burned themselves to death between 1963 and 1975, to protest the anti-Buddhist policies pursued by the government of South Vietnam. The "autocremation" of Thich Quang Duc on 11 June, 1963 was captured by an American reporter in a series of photographs. This created a world-wide alarm.

7.31 Major developments took place in South Vietnam during the war-years. The Vietnamese Unified Buddhist Church was founded. Also, Van Hanh University, the first Buddhist University, was established in Saigon. Eminent monks such as Thich Tri Quang and Thich Tam Chau became household names. The School of Youth for Social Service at Van Hanh University was founded by Thich Nhat Hanh (born in 1926), who coined the term "Engaged Buddhism" to refer to the kind of Buddhism that he wanted to see develop: one that would actively and directly concern itself with the welfare of the people.

7.32 Thich Nhat Hanh was one of the leaders of the "Struggle Movement" or "Third Way" that tried to bring the War to an end without taking sides with either the North or the South. He went to the West as a spokesperson for the Buddhist antiwar perspective, but somehow he was unable to return home. Like him, many Vietnamese refugees migrated to Europe or North America.

7.33 Thich Nhat Hanh and his associates took refuge in Paris, France, where they established, in the 1970's, the Sweet Potato Farm Community. Subsequently, in 1982, they established Plum Village in southwestern France. Thich Nhat Hanh has since become a world-renowned "Engaged Buddhist'. Among his associates, the most well-known is Sister Chan Khong.

Other Vietnamese scholars in the West

7.34 Thich Thien - An came to USA in 1966 as a visiting professor at UCLA and taught traditional Thien meditation. In 1975, he published "Buddhism and Zen in Vietnam".

Taiwan

7.35 Although Buddhism reached Taiwan only in the latter half of the seventeenth century, the people of this island have taken significant steps, since then, to implement the social message. Upto the middle of the seventeenth century, Taiwan was viewed by the mainland Chinese as a land of pirates, typhoons, plagues, and headhunting natives, In 1662, when the Chinese failed to restore the fallen Ming dynasty, Taiwan proved to be a convenient place to escape to.

7.36 The Dutch colonial rulers controlled Taiwan from 1624 until 1663, when Cheng Chan-Kung forced them to leave. The son of the new Taiwanese leader, named Cheng Ching, established the first Buddhist temple in Taiwan. In 1675, a Taiwanese military commander, named Chen Yonghua, built a monastery called the Dragon Lake Grotto, and he invited a Chinese monk (named Canche) to serve as abbot at this monastery. Subequently, Canche founded another monastery "The Blue Cloud Monastery".

7.37 As the island became more settled, many more monasteries were established. Despite this vigorous activity, most of the monks and nuns in these monasteries had probably received only the novices' ordination because there was no ordaining monastery in Taiwan and only a few of the monks journeyed to the mainland to receive the full precepts.

7.38 In 1895, the Chinese government ceded the island to Japan, and the Japanese troops brought Buddhist chaplains with them. These chaplains were eager to establish mission stations in order to propagate Japanese Buddhism to the native population, but funding from their head temples in Japan was insufficient, and only a very small percentage of the Chinese population of the island ever unrolled in Japanese Buddhist missions.

7.39 The Japanese colonial period lasted till 1945. The fifty year period (1895-1945) saw the institution of the first facilities for transmitting the full monastic precepts in Taiwan. Most of the island's Buddhist temples affiliated themselves with one of the three central temples:

(i) North : Yueh-mei Mountain temple

(ii) Center : Fa-yun temple

(iii) South : Kai-yuan temple

7.40 The Japanese rulers tried to introduce, on the island, the system of "married priesthood" (as was the practice in Japan). However, the Taiwanese Buddhists refused to accept this.

7.41 The Japanese administration did achieve an institutional success, viz. that clergy and laity joined together to form Buddhist organizations that functioned as government liaisons. Under this scheme, several organizations were formed, of which the largest one was "South Seas Buddhist Association". This scheme was discontinued in 1945, because the "Vegetarian religion" group of laypeople wanted to maintain their own independent status, in spite of opposition from monastic groups.

7.42 Political developments of the years 1945-1949 created new problems. In 1945, Taiwan was returned to Mainland Chinese Nationalistic government, which, in 1949, was defeated by the communists. A number of Buddhist monks from the mainland fled to Taiwan alongside Chiang Kai-Shek's military personnel, who hoped (in vain) to use Taiwan as a base of operations until they could return to the mainland to re-build the old system.

7.43 For a few years after 1949, the government in Taiwan controlled Buddhist activities, by assigning a regulatory role to "Buddhist Association of the Republic of China" (BAROC). This created problems, like the non-availability of confiscated Japanese era monasteries for religious use, and the government's obstruction of efforts to establish a

Buddhist university. However, government control was gradually relaxed from 1960 onward, leading to the establishment of independent Buddhist organizations in Taiwan. This policy-change enabled Cheng Yen, a nun who was ordained by Yin shun of mainland China (reference para 5.50) to expand her activities. She later founded Tzu Chi, Taiwan's most important charity organization. Tzu Chi runs several hospitals in Taiwan, and conducts worldwide relief work. A 1999 earthquake centered in Puli brought praise for Tzu Chi for its effective response.

7.44 During the 1980's, Buddhist leaders pressed Taiwan's Ministry of Education to relax various policies that prevented the organization of a Buddhist university. The eventual result was that in the 1990's, not one but half a dozen educational institutions emerged, each associated with a different Buddhist leader. Among them were Tzu Chi university, Hsuan-chuang university, Huafan university, Fo Guang university, Nenhua university, and Dharma Drum Buddhist College.

7.45 In 2001, Master Hsin Tao of Ling Jiou Shan opened the Museum of World Religions in Taiwan. In additon to exhibits on ten different religions of the world, the museum also offered "Avatamsaka World", a model illustrating the Avatamsaka Sutra.

7.46 Several of the Buddhist leaders of Taiwan have taken steps to implement the social message of Mahayana. For example, Xingyun has published his vision of "Fo Kuang Buddhism", in which he seeks to turn followers' attention away from otherworldly concerns, such as rituals for the dead and rebirth in the Pure Land, and toward efforts to benefit living beings in this world, Similarly, Zhengyan, founder of the Buddhist Compassionate Relief Tzu-Chi Association, trains the followers to be of assistance to needy people in the world. As an association composed almost entirely of lay people, the focus is on social action rather than maintaining monastic roles. Individual monasteries such as the Nongchan Monastery in northern Taipei and the Faguang Monastery in downtown Taipei no longer use disposable chapsticks and bowls due to a concern for the environment. In all these efforts, the slogan is "to build a Pure Land on Earth".

CHAPTER 8

Mahayana Intermingled with other Doctrines in Nepal and Tibet

8.1 In this chapter we shall briefly describe how the people of Nepal and Tibet welcomed Mahayana Buddhism along with other doctrines. Although the presence of other doctrines was likely to have a negative effect on the process of implementation of Mahayana's social message, a positive and balancing factor operating at the same time was the availability of Shantideva's inspiring book "Bodhicaryavatara". Whether the net result has been positive or negative, it is for the readers to judge, but we will present the relevant facts, first in regard to Nepal, and next, in regard to Tibet.

Nepal

8.2 Nepal as a separate country came into existence in 1769. Prior to that, it was a northern region of India. Therefore, Mahayana texts were available to Nepalese people, automatically, and there were no language problems, because Sanskrit was known to them.

8.3 Around the year 1300, after Nalanda University was destroyed by Muslim invaders, many Buddhist scholars moved to Nepal, along with Sanskrit texts. This made Nepal an important center of Buddhist scholarship.

8.4 From the viewpoint of the spreading of the social message of Mahayana, Nepal was fortunate to have Shantideva's

"Bodhicaryavatara". This put Nepal in a relatively advantageous position, compared with countries of East Asia where "Bodhicaryavatara" was not available. Researchers have found out that "Nepal Bhasa scholars" made available to people, local language translation of the Lotus Sutra as well as of Bodhicaryavatara.

8.5 These were the "positive" points. The most imporant negative point was that Vajrayana Buddhism (also known as Tantra) reached Nepal. As the Arhat is the ideal of Theravada, and Bodhisattva is the ideal of Mahayana, so Mahasiddha is the ideal of Tantra. A Mahasiddha is believed to possess extraordinary capability, therefore he (as a guru) can use unconventional methods while giving spiritual training to his disciples. Some of these methods might appear to be unhygienic or even unethical. A Mahasiddha is often supposed to be able to perform magical feats or miracles. Obviously, such features of Vajrayana (or Tantra) can prove to be obstacles in the path of implementing the social message of Mahayana.

8.6 The presence of Vajrayana in Nepal was not only due to the Indian influence, but also because it came to Nepal as a part of Tibetan Buddhism. Researchers have found out that, during the fourteenth century, many Tibetan monks came to the Nepal valley to obtain Tantric texts. Some of them also established branch monasteries affiliated with the main Tibetan monastery—the first such monasteries were located near the monumental stupas at Svayambhu and Bauddha.

8.7 During the twentieth century, when Dalai Lama left Tibet and moved to India, a large number of Tibetan refugees moved to Nepal. There they have been building various institutions for their community. Since Tibetan Buddhism has become increasingly attractive to Westerners, many Tibetan lamas have established "dharma centers" that in most ways resemble traditional monasteries. Here one can find textual study as well as meditation being pursued by both ethnic Tibetans and Westerners clad in monastic robes.

8.8 Buddhists in Nepal constitute nearly 11 percent of the population, the rest being mostly Hindus. The two communities maintain cordial relations with each other. In 2006, Nepal became a secular country where all religions have equal opportunities and freedom to live peacefully.

Tibet

8.9 Tibetan literature attributes the formal introduction of Buddhism into the country, to the reign of its first emperor, during the first half of the seventh century. One of the wives of the emperor was from Nepal, and another from China. These women are credited with constructing the temples of "Magical Appearance". The emperor himself is credited with having one of his ministers create the Tibetan alphabet from an Indian script and write the first grammar.

8.10 The first Buddhist monastery in Tibet was built around the year 780. Many monks from India as well as China came to Tibet at that time. An important Indian monk, Santaraksita, ordained the first group of Tibetans. Another Indian guru, Padmasambhava, was a Tantric, whose inspiration became important later, in making Tantra a prominent part of Tibetan Buddhism.

8.11 Translation bureaus were opened by Tibetan emperors during the eighth and ninth centuries. While the official bureaus were busy with the Mahayana texts, unofficial translators tended to feature tantric works. A council was therefore convened to regularize the translation activity. The result was the emergence of classical Tibetan, a literary language developed to render both sophisticated Buddhist terminology and foreign political documents into the rapidly evolving Tibetan medium.

8.12 Translations were initially made from Sanskrit as well as Chinese, causing tension between Indian and Chinese scholars. In the year 794, a series of discussions took place between all the experts, who ultimately gave their verdict in favor of Sanskrit. From then on, translations from Chinese were discontinued.

8.13 But the steady progress that was being made suffered a jolt, during the years 838-842 when the last of the emperors began a campaign of suppression of Buddhism. The situation became really complicated when the emperor was assassinated by a Buddhist monk. Disagreement over imperial succession led to the fragmentation of the Tibetan empire. The period from 850 to 950 was a chaotic time marked by popular revolts and warlordism. Surviving Buddhist monks fled, and monastic practice practically came to a halt for almost one hundred years.

8.14 When the situation stabilized, the king of West Tibet invited, in 1042, the Indian missionary, Atisha, who introduced the "triple discipline", that is, monastic, Mahayana, and Tantra, all three intermingled. At the same time, Atisha promoted Shantideva's book "Bodhicaryavatara". Atisha's mission left a long-lasting imprint on the form of Tibetan Buddhism.

8.15 The Tibetan religious landscape changed dramatically in the seventeenth century. The Fifth Dalai Lama (affectionately known to Tibetans as the Great Fifth), used the military might of the Mongols to solidify his control over Tibet. In this way, in the year 1642, the reign of the Dalai Lamas was regularized.

8.16 By the turn of the twentieth century, Tibetans were being exposed to the wider world, especially through the Younghusband expedition of 1904. The British Government used their superior military strength, and the Chinese were forced to accept a British Trade Agent stationed in Tibet.

8.17 Prior to the establishment of the communist government in China, the Dalai Lama held supreme religious as well as political power over Tibet. Of course, since the Dalai Lama spent most of his time in religious study, meditation, and guidance to practitioners, he wanted the Kashag (or advisory council) to take care of political matters. The Kashag consisted of monks as well as laymen, their shares being equal. Tibetan women never held responsible positions in political matters.

8.18 The present Dalai Lama (who is number 14 in the lineage) was only 14 years of age (in 1949) when the communist government came to power in China. His formal recognition as 14th Dalai Lama took place in 1950 when he was 15. Although the People's Republic of China wanted to assert control over Tibet, they decided to do so gradually. So they formulated a "Seventeen-point agreement" to establish a joint communist-Lamaist administration over Tibet.

8.19 However, the Dalai Lama felt that this "Agreement" was only on paper, to avoid criticism at the international level. Therefore, in 1959, he fled to India. The Government of India welcomed him as the religious head of Tibet. Ever since then, the Dalai Lama is operating from Dharamsala in India.

8.20 While explaining his religious views, Dalai Lama has quoted from Bodhicaryavatara, and acknowledged that he was inspired by this book. It is obvious that he has accepted the social message of Mahayana Buddhism. But since he is away from Tibet, he is unable to implement the social message in respect of the people residing in that country. Dalai Lama's contribution at the international level is so well known that we do not consider it neccssary to write about it in this book.

CHAPTER 9

Summary of the Book and Concluding Remarks

Summary of the Book

9.1 Chapter One states the primary purpose of the book to be: firstly, to share with the readers, selected passages from the Lotus Sutra and Bodhicaryavatara, which, in our opinion, give the social message of Mahayana Buddhism, and secondly, to give the methods of implementing the social message. Furthermore, a subsidiary purpose of the book is stated to be: to review briefly what the Mahayana-influenced Asian countries have done by way of follow-up action.

9.2 Chapter Two starts with the recognition that the basic source of the social message of Mahayana Buddhism is "The Lotus Sutra". Although the exact date of preparation of this text (in India) is not known, it is generally believed to have been written during the first two centuries. Subsequently, during the eighth century, the social message was elaborated by Shantideva in his book "Bodhicaryavatara". The joint utilization of these two books ensures that we obtain a demystified and comprehensive account of the meaning, scope, and methods of implementation of the social message of Mahayana. A Chapter-wise outline of the contents of both the books is also given in Chapter Two.

9.3 Chapter Three, specifying the social message of Mahayana, is the heart of the book. In the opinion of the book's authors, the social message of Mahayana is : Contribute to the good of the world, the complete meaning of which is obtained by looking at the message together with four sub-messages :-

(i) Bodhisattva-based ideal.

Bodhisattva, rather than Arhat or Pratyekabuddha, should be the ideal to be attained in human life, because Bodhisattva's aim is "good of the world". "Concentration on Bodhisattva" is the "eka-yana" (Single Vehicle) of Mahayana Buddhism.

(ii) Spiritual as well as Secular

The "good of the world" includes spiritual advancement of all as well as satisfaction of their basic needs like food, health and education.

(iii) No discrimination

All human beings should have the assurance of equality of treatment, free from discrimination on any ground like sex, age and socio-economic status. In particular, the status of women, in regard to their education, health, and participation in religion, should be equal to that of men.

(iv) Reform rather than punish

Wherever evil-minded, anti-social persons exist in the society, they should be reformed rather than punished. This means adherence to Ahimsa (non-violence).

9.4 For the message, as well as for each of the four sub-messages, relevant portions of the two books are given in Chapter 3. This presentation includes the text in Sanskrit and its simple meaning in English.

9.5 Chapter Four is the longest chapter of the book because it presents those portions (and these are quite substantial portions) of the two books which give instructions to people about the methods of implementing the social message. Keeping in mind the importance of tackling different types of implementational problems, we have adopted the following five-way classification of methods:-

(a) Spreading the message

(b) Motivation and inspiration

(c) Non-violent action and perseverance

(d) Worship and prayer

(e) Meditation and dedication

9.6 An important point about the methods of implementing the message is, that the section presenting "non-violent action and perseverance" is the longest of the five sections. Obviously, the Mahayana scriptures stressed the practical aspects of their teachings.

9.7 Chapters Five to Eight present a short "historical review" of what the Mahayana-influenced Asian countries – China, Japan, Korea, Vietnam, Taiwan, Nepal, Tibet – have done by way of follow-up action. Detailed country-wise studies have been made by many authors, and immense literature is available, so our task is limited to showing what a heroic journey it has been, in each of the seven countries. We have tried to give a selective presentation for each country, upto the emergence of the wonderful phenomenon of "engaged Buddhism" – but we have not considered it necessary to write in detail about "engaged Buddhists" because their contribution at the international level is so well known.

Concluding remarks

9.8 We as researchers specializing in modern trends in Hinduism and Buddhism, have earlier made an in-depth study of Bhagavad - Gita, and on the same pattern, have now made an in-depth study of the Lotus Sutra and Bodhicaryavatara. We have noticed that the social message: "Contribute to the good of the world" is the same, in the Bhagavad-Gita, on the one hand, and in the two Mahayana texts, on the other. The Sanskrit words used in the Bhagavad-Gita are (i) lokasamgraha and (ii) sarvabhutahitam. The corresponding words in the Mahayana-texts are (a) loka-hitam and (b) sarvasattvasukham.

9.9 Of the four sub-messages, the first one is "Bodhisattva-based ideal". The corresponding expression in Bhagavad-Gita is "Jivanmukta-based ideal". The characteristic features of "Bodhisattva" and "Jivan-mukta" are practically the same.

9.10 The second sub-message is "Spiritual as well as secular". The corresponding expressions in Bhagavad-Gita are "Atmoddhara and sarira-yatra", meaning "spiritual uplift and satisfaction of basic needs."

9.11 The third sub-message is "No discrimination". The corresponding expression in Bhagavad-Gita is "Samadristi" meaning "equal vision."

9.12 The fourth sub-message is "Reform rather than punish." The corresponding expression in Bhagavad-Gita is "Ahimsa" meaning "non-violence."

9.13 Next, of the five methods of implementing the message, the first one is "Spreading the message." Since Hinduism is not a missionary religion, there is no corresponding expression in Bhagavad-Gita.

9.14 The second method is "Motivation and inspiration." The corresponding expression in Bhagavad-Gita is "Buddhi-Yoga and Jnana-yoga" meaning "the way of intellect and knowledge."

9.15 The third method is "Non-violent action and perseverance." The corresponding expression in Bhagavad-Gita is "Karma-yoga" meaning "way of action". In fact, the word "Karma-Yogin" can be considered as equivalent to "engaged Buddhist."

9.16 The fourth method is "Worship and prayer." The corresponding expression in Bhagavad-Gita is "Bhakti-yoga" meaning " way of devotion."

9.17 The fifth method is "Meditation and dedication". The corresponding expression in Bhagavad-Gita is "Dhyana-yoga" meaning "way of meditation."

Select Bibliography

1. The internet proved to be a very valuable source. "Digital Sanskrit Buddhist Canon" has Buddhist Sanskrit texts, edited by Dr. P.L. Vaidya. "Saddharmapundarikasutram" is No. 6 in the series. "Bodhicaryavatara" is No. 12 in the series.

2. "Sacred Books of the East" edited by F. Max Muller are available in fifty volumes. Volume 21 is "Saddharmapundarika or Lotus of the True Laws", translated from Sanskrit to English by Jan Hendrik Kern, initially published by Clarendon Press (Oxford) in 1884, reprinted by Motilal Banarsidass Publishers, Delhi, eight times between 1965 and 2006.

3. Buddhist Mahayana Texts, Vol. 49 of the Sacred Books of the East. Originally published by Oxford University Press, 1894, reprinted eight times by Motilal Banarsidass Publishers, Delhi, between 1965 and 2006.

4. "Bodhicaryavatara" translated from Sanskrit to English by Marion L. Matics was first published in UK in 1971, under the title "Entering the Path of Enlightenment" by George Allen and Unwin, reprinted by Motilal Banarsidass Publishers, Delhi, 2007.

5. Soka Gakkai brought out in 1993, "The Lotus Sutra", translated from Chinese to English by Burton Watson, and printed at Columbia University Press.

6. Tenzin Gyatso (14th Dalai Lama) wrote a commentary on Bodhicaryavatara under the title "A Flash of Lightning in the Dark of Night: A Guide to the Bodhisattva's Way of Life", published by Shambhala, Boston, 1994.

7. S. Batchelor's "A Guide to the Bodhisattva's Way of Life", brought out by Dharamsala : Library of Tibetan Works and Archives, 1979.

8. Encyclopedia of Buddhism, edited by Robert E. Buswell, brought out by Macmillan Reference USA and Thomson–Gale, 2004, 2 volumes.

9. The A to Z of Buddhism, by Carl Olson, brought out by The Scarecrow Press, Plymonth, UK, 2009.

10. The Bhagavad–Gita by S.Radhakrishnan, Harper and Row, New York, 1973.

11. The Social Role of the Gita : How and Why, by Satya P. Agarwal, brought out by Motilal Banarsidass, Delhi, 1993.

Index

References are to paragraph numbers, not to pages